BUILDING CATHEDRALS
The Power of Purpose

Greg Coker

with Terry Daniels, Dave Tatman and Skip Wirth
Illustrations by Faye Christian Phillips

Foreword by
Captain Charles Plumb USNR (Ret.)
FORMER NAVY FIGHTER PILOT, POW

clark legacies
Published by **Clark Legacies**,
an imprint of
Integrated Media Corporation
12305 Westport Road - Suite 4
Louisville, Kentucky 40245

Printed in the U.S.A.
10 9 8 7 6 5 4 3 2 1

ISBN: 978-1-58374-277-8

CONTENTS

DEVELOPING A"LIFE OF PURPOSE"

CONCLUSION

THE
STORY

Christopher Wren is known in England as one of the greatest architects in history.

He was commissioned to rebuild Saint Paul's Cathedral after the Great Fire of 1666, which destroyed London.

One day, while rebuilding St. Paul's Cathedral, Christopher Wren observed three bricklayers on a scaffold: one crouched, one half-standing, and one standing very tall, working very hard and fast.

To the first bricklayer, Christopher Wren asked the question, "What are you doing?" to which the bricklayer replied, "I'm working."

The second bricklayer, when asked the question, "What are you doing?" responded, "I'm building a wall."

But the third bricklayer, when Christopher Wren asked the question, "What are you doing?" responded with a gleam in his eye, "I'm building a cathedral to The Almighty."

FOREWORD

Ifirst met Greg Coker when I spoke to a group of executives almost 20 years ago. My speech was titled "Leadership in Adversity." I was flattered when we reconnected, and he let me know how a metaphor that I had introduced that day continued to provide purpose and meaning in his life. Little did I know he would return the favor with an equally powerful metaphor and an invitation to write the Foreword for this inspirational book. What you have in your hands is a classic story that has been told for over 300 years. And while you may have heard some version of this story, surprisingly no one has taken the time like Greg Coker and asked a few simple but powerful questions: specifically, "What can we learn from the characters in this powerful illustration of purpose?" and "What are the modern day applications in our lives?" The metaphors are not only descriptive, they are cathartic. They are captivating. As I read this book, I experienced a wide range of emotions, but most importantly I was inspired to live better, to love more and to become more aware and more appreciative of the "Cathedral Builders" in my life, both past and present.

One of the Cathedral Builders in my life was a US Navy sailor I accidentally met several years after he had saved my life. I was sitting in a restaurant in Kansas City as a man about two tables away kept looking over at me. I didn't recognize him. A few minutes into our meal he stood up, walked over to my table, looked down at me, pointed his finger in my face and said, "You're Captain Plumb."

I looked up and said, "Yes, I'm Captain Plumb."

He said, "You flew jet fighters in Vietnam. You were on the aircraft carrier *Kitty Hawk*. You were shot down. You parachuted into enemy hands and spent six years as a prisoner of war."

I said, "How in the world did you know all that?"

He replied, "Because I packed your parachute!"

Well, for a guy who travels the world speaking, I found myself speechless! I staggered to my feet and held out a very grateful hand of thanks. This guy came up with the perfect response. He grabbed my hand, pumped my arm and said, "I guess it worked!"

"Indeed it did, my friend," I said. "And I must tell you, I've said many prayers of thanks for your nimble fingers, but I never thought I'd have the opportunity to express my gratitude in person."

He asked, "Were all the panels there?"

"Well," I said, "I must be honest—of the eighteen panels in that parachute, I had fifteen good ones. Three were torn, but it wasn't your fault, it was mine. I jumped out of that jet fighter at a high rate of speed, and very close to the ground. That's what tore the panels in the chute. It wasn't the way you packed it."

"Now, let me ask you a question," I said. "Do you keep track of all the parachutes you've packed?" Now, what follows is perhaps the most significant part of the story and illustrates the power of Building Cathedrals.

"No," he responded. "It's enough gratification for me just to know that I've served," responded the man who packed my parachute.

I didn't get much sleep that night. I kept thinking about that man. I kept wondering what he might have looked like in a Navy uniform: bib in the back, bell-bottom trousers, and a Dixie Cup hat. I wondered how many times I might have passed him on board the *Kitty Hawk*. I wondered how many times I might have seen him and not even said "Good morning," or "How are you?" or anything. You see, I was a fighter pilot and he was just a sailor. But how many hours did that sailor spend at that long wooden table in the bowels of that ship, weaving the shrouds and folding the silks of those life-saving parachutes? I'm ashamed to admit that at the time, I could not have cared less—until one day my parachute came along and he packed it for me! I had made the assumption that he and the other 5,000 men aboard that ship were simply "Bricklayers" when in fact, they were "Cathedral Builders!"

So before you jump into reading this book, let me ask you: How's your "parachute packing" coming along? Who looks to you for strength in times of need? And perhaps, more importantly, who are the special people in your life who provide the encouragement you need when the chips are down? Perhaps it's time right now to give those people a call and thank them for packing your parachute. I needed a variety of "parachutes" when my plane was shot down over enemy territory—I needed a physical parachute, a mental parachute, an emotional parachute, and most importantly, a spiritual parachute.

I'm often asked, "How did you do it, Commander? How did you survive six years in a prisoner of war camp? I could have never done it."

My answer is always, "Of course you could." My secret for enduring six years of hell is really not a secret at all. First and foremost, I had faith in an omniscient God, knowing that His will would be done. I never doubted that I could persevere; I simply trusted God's promise to answer my prayers. I also loved my country, its people, and its freedoms. I realized that, because of the human element, mistakes could be made. But in growing up I had discerned that most of the people in this great land are honorable and compassionate; if it had not been so, I would not have accepted the commission to protect these ideals.

Second, I had self-discipline. It would have been easier to avoid torture by succumbing to my captors' interrogations. It would have been easier to assume helplessness by blaming an evil world. I could have rationalized myself into mental and physical paralysis. Quite simply, I could have just simply "laid the bricks." However, strict self-obedience gave me the ability to persevere.

Third, I had pride. I was proud to know an omnipotent God. I was then and continue to be proud of my country and its heritage. I was proud of my family. I was proud of myself.

And finally, like you and the people you will meet in the following pages, I had a Cathedral to build!

Captain J. Charles Plumb, USNR (Ret.)

Professional Speaker

Author, *I'm No Hero*

www.charlieplumb.com

Questions for Consideration

- Who in your life has "packed your parachute"?
- What key "panels" are in your parachute?
- Whose parachute have you packed?
- What positive events have occurred in your life as a result of your packing someone else's parachute?
- What negative events?
- What have you learned from these events about yourself?
- What panels have you found most critical in packing others' parachutes?
- Whose parachute could you be packing?
- How would you describe the condition of your parachutes? (Your physical parachute? Your mental parachute? Your emotional parachute? And most importantly, your spiritual parachute?)

ACKNOWLEDGMENTS

I thank God for giving me the inspiration to write this book, the perseverance to keep on keeping on, even when the "Bricklayer" in me said that I couldn't, I shouldn't, and questioned who was I to think I could write a book? I thank God for the ideas and the people that entered both my mind and my life during the writing of this book. I thank my supportive wife, who constantly reminded me while I was consumed with writing this book, delivering the speech, and conducting workshops across the country, that my personal "Cathedral," the most important "Cathedral," was God, our marriage, and our children, not this book, not the speech. Well said!

Thank you to the contributing authors Terry Daniels, Dave Tatman and Skip Wirth. From the first time I met Terry Daniels, heard him preach at Loving Chapel Church, and discovered his vast private sector experience, I knew he had to be part of this project.

The day I toured the Corvette plant, General Motors' flagship manufacturing facility, I heard plant manager Dave Tatman declare, "We don't build cars; we build dreams." As I witnessed firsthand how employees and community leaders responded to his inspirational leadership, I knew that not only had I discovered a modern day "Christopher Wren," but also that he would play an integral part in this book.

Thanks to Skip Wirth, who sat at Panera Bread and coached me through one of the most devastating of all personal fires, a job loss. I knew his vast knowledge, experience and insight on stress management had to be a part of this book.

To Faye Christian Phillips, a wonderful illustrator, a true Cathedral Builder and a beautiful person. Thank you, my friend.

I thank Bobby Clark with Clark Legacies, LLC for providing the tools and the avenue for Dave, Terry, Skip and me to build a Cathedral and share it with others.

And thanks to the people you will meet in the following pages for inviting me into their hearts and allowing me to tell their stories. I have never been more touched and felt the Holy Spirit more strongly as I spent time with these Cathedral Builders. It is both an honor and a blessing to share their stories with you.

To Captain Charlie Plumb (Ret.), General Dan Cherry (Ret.), General Carmen Cavezza (Ret.) and Matthew Young: I have never been more proud to be an American and never felt more indebted to the millions of men and women who are serving and have served our great nation in the Armed Services. Thank you for allowing me to share your story. Like the Cathedral Builders of long ago, the people you will read about in the following pages share a single desire: to create something of purpose, something that endures.

Greg Coker

"Where there is no vision, the people perish."
—Proverbs 29:18

INTRODUCTION

It was March 2008 and after several hours, I convinced myself the right thing to do was to stop by the funeral home and console a friend whose father had died. The funeral home was crowded and while I waited to pay my condolences, I couldn't help but notice a rather thick book resting beside several family photos on a coffee table. Not really sure what it was and wanting to pass the time, I opened it and began to read. It was a journal that my friend's father had kept since his early 20s.

I conveyed my condolences to the family but was preoccupied with what I had just read. I was inspired and deeply touched, inspired by the detail of his stories and recollection of key events, many that I had witnessed having grown up with his son. I was inspired to tell my story and encourage others to tell their story. I was inspired to touch others; inspired to demystify the process of writing and sharing one's thoughts, philosophies and life lessons. I was inspired to leave a legacy.

That night I started to write. And wherever I went, a legal pad was always by my side, from the front seat of my car to the many hotel room nightstands. After a few months, my stories started to take shape. I started sharing with family, friends and business associates and soon my excitement and passion led to invitations to speak to local civic clubs, businesses, school systems and non-profit organizations.

One story that transfixed all audiences was a story that I had told for many years as an illustration of the power of purpose. Early on I did not know the origin of the story, or even if it were true. Then I learned that the story is attributed to Christopher Wren, as told at the beginning of the book. And while this story has always captivated audiences, it had begun to convict me.

For most of my career I had considered myself a Cathedral Builder. But now at 47 years old, after spending the last 20 plus years striving for "success," I felt like I lacked significance. In fact,

I was feeling more like a "Bricklayer," becoming more and more frustrated, more and more disengaged. And the more I gave this speech and told this story, the more I realized I was not alone.

Numerous studies report that less than half of employees are actually satisfied with their jobs. Other surveys suggest that a high number of employees would leave their companies today if the economy were better. And with one in ten Americans currently unemployed, six of those ten unemployed say the next job they get will most likely not be the one they want; instead, they expect to have to settle for an alternative. (*USA Today*/Gallop, Dec. 21, 2010—Jan. 9, 2011.) Even if we are working, three out of four adult Americans have a family member or close friend who has experienced a job loss, which creates stress, worry and concern for everyone.

A women and workplace survey from *More Magazine* revealed that 43% of the women surveyed say they are less ambitious now than they were a decade ago. And only a quarter of the 500 women ages 35 to 60 say they're working toward their next promotion. Three out of four women in the survey, 73%, say they would not apply for their boss' job, reporting that the stress, office politics and lack of significance make the leap simply not worth it. In fact, two of three women said they would accept considerably less money for more free time and more flexibility. The bottom line is, there's never been a time when Americans, both male and female, young and old, were more in need of a sense of purpose—significance in addition to success. In short, we're all looking for a Cathedral to build.

Armed with the images of Christopher Wren, the fire of 1666 and the three bricklayers with whom most can relate, this story went from simply captivating audiences to convicting audiences as it had convicted me. I had found the perfect metaphor for what others were feeling and needing in their lives to give them a sense of purpose. Most importantly, I had found my Cathedral. I had discovered an ideal leader in Christopher Wren. The Great Fire of 1666, which leveled London, provided the perfect metaphor for our personal heartaches, setbacks and tragedies, which we must overcome in order to be Cathedral Builders.

The first bricklayer represents way too many of us who simply show up to work lacking any real purpose, vision, or inspiration. The second bricklayer, who could at least see the wall, represents an opportunity to transition from "just showing up" to seeing the big picture. The dynamics between the three bricklayers cannot be overlooked or underestimated. The third bricklayer in the story, the Cathedral Builder, provides the inspiration, importance, and motivation to never lose sight of the "big picture."

Like many of you, I've played each character; I've lived each metaphor. I've been Christopher Wren, leaving the comfort of a corporate office and traveling thousands of miles simply to convey how important each and every employee was in achieving the company mission. At various times in my life, I've been each of the Bricklayers. And during the writing of this book, one Friday afternoon at 3:30 PM in my boss's office, I immediately started to smell the metaphorical smoke and began to prepare for the "fire" that would indeed be devastating. Interestingly, my last day with this particular employer was September 2nd. Take a guess what day the Great Fire of 1666 occurred. You guessed it, September 2nd. But little did I know that when I embarked on writing this book, it would not only be my Cathedral, but also it would be the inspiration, the metaphor and the strength for rebuilding my life, just as London rebuilt after that devastating day in 1666.

I hope that Terry Daniels, Dave Tatman, Skip Wirth and I play a part in inspiring you to tell your story, to write your story. We hope you never underestimate the amazing power and responsibility you have to touch and inspire others. We hope and pray you never miss an opportunity to tell that cleaning person at your workplace how great everything looks and how what they do indeed makes a difference. But most of all we hope and pray that you will find, that you will pursue, and that you will never give up on building your Cathedral.

Questions for Consideration

- What key moments, both positive and negative, have drastically impacted your life? Do you keep a journal? If not, should you?
- If you started to write your own story, where would you begin?
- How would you rate your career or job satisfaction?
- Overall, how do you feel your employees/team members would rate their job satisfaction?
- Do you feel that your current career/job aligns with your sense of purpose?
- To which character in the story can you most relate? Why?
- Do you recognize and support others in the building of their Cathedrals? If so, how?

CHRISTOPHER WREN

Clever men like Christopher Wren

Only occur just now and then

No one expects in perpetuity

Architects of his ingenuity;

No, never a cleverer dipped his pen

Than clever Sir Christopher.

Christopher Wren.

—Hugh Chesterman

Sir Christopher Wren was born October 20, 1632 into a very prominent family. His father was a well-educated man holding the position of Dean of Windsor. His mother inherited her family's estate shortly before dying at an early age. Wren had several siblings who would die within a few weeks of their birth, leaving him to be raised by his father and an older sister. As a child, Christopher Wren was small in stature and frail. From an early age he loved to draw and was fascinated with science. While educated at Westminster, it was Wren's uncle, a mathematician, who had a profound influence, tutoring as well as encouraging him to experiment with astronomy.

After Westminster, he did not immediately continue his formal education but instead studied science by working with Dr. Thomas Willis, known as the father of neurology. Wren assisted him with several anatomical experiments and created models to illustrate how certain muscles worked in the brain. These illustrations actually appeared in medical journals and textbooks up until the early 1900s.

It is believed that one of Christopher Wren's earliest and most undocumented accomplishments was being the first to inject medicine intravenously. Wren injected wine into a dog's vein and observed visible signs of intoxication. Amazingly, this was only a few years before scientists realized that blood actually circulated through our bodies. There is also strong evidence that Wren may have provided many of the great advances in brain surgery credited to Dr. Thomas Willis. Additionally, neurosurgeon/historian John Fulton of Yale University credited Sir Christopher Wren with having discovered the importance of antiseptic agents.

Wren entered Wadham College in 1649 receiving a B.A. degree, and he later earned an M.A. from Oxford in 1653. While on faculty at Oxford University, he brought to astronomy a talent for the use of geometry. Sir Isaac Newton called Wren a leader in that field. At Oxford, Wren not only carried out many scientific experiments, but also made significant contributions to mathematics and to the field of optics by publishing a description of a machine to create drawings of lenses and mirrors. Christopher Wren had a wide breadth of other interests that ranged from inventing military devices to machines that lifted water.

While a professor of astronomy at Gresham College in London, Wren even used astronomical arguments to defend accounts of phenomena recounted in the Bible. Because of Wren's modesty, we generally don't hear much of his scientific work. He didn't patent or seek credit for most of his work, and when one scientist beat him to a publication of the explanation of Saturn's rings, Christopher Wren simply said, "I was fond of his work and enjoyed reading it."

Wren shared his many talents by founding the Royal Society of London, a prestigious scientific think tank. Wren's interest in architecture may have begun during his Oxford days designing military devices to protect cities and ports, but he is most remembered for the opportunity that came with the rebuilding after the fire of 1666. During this time Wren took center stage, after being appointed King's Surveyor. He planned the entire city of London and rebuilt over 50 churches.

Christopher Wren is best known for being the architect of St. Paul's Cathedral, but his first design was actually rejected by London's city council for not being grand enough. His second proposal was rejected by the clergy for not keeping with the proper form of the Christian church. The third design was accepted when he was 43 years old, and work progressed over a 35 year period, giving him a chance to see its completion a full 12 years before his death at 90. Interestingly, the life expectancy in the 1600s was only 43. The power of purpose certainly had a positive effect on Christopher Wren!

While Wren enjoyed much success, he was no stranger to personal devastation and experienced many of his own personal fires. In addition to the death of his mother and several siblings at early ages, Wren's first wife would also die young. Although he remarried, that marriage would last only six years, as his second wife died shortly after giving birth. Professionally, the road to success was not without conflict and personal persecution. In the book, *Sir Christopher Wren, Scientist, Scholar and Architect,* Lawrence Weaver recalls how Wren was treated with incredible meanness by a less than supportive city commission. The brilliant architect was thwarted at every turn during the rebuilding of St. Paul's Cathedral, receiving only a meager salary that at one point was suspended, and was often in arrears.

Wren avoided taking any personal credit for his work, and upon his retirement he proclaimed, "If I glory, it is in the singular mercy of God, who has enabled me to begin and finish my great work." Persecution pursued him to the grave, giving his son the unique opportunity of presenting an immortal epitaph. A more fitting memorial had been suggested but rejected by authorities, so Wren was buried in a simple crypt below St. Paul's Cathedral. His son, seeking to explain the absence of a proper memorial in the location of his father's greatest triumph, wrote on the plain tablet marking his resting place, one of the most famous epitaphs of all times: "LECTOR SI MONUMEENTUM REQUIRIS: CIRCUMSPICE," which translates as "If you seek his monument, look around."

Questions for Consideration

- What characteristics of Christopher Wren do you find most intriguing? Why?
- What skills/attributes do you feel best served Wren in his success? Why?
- What leadership skills do you feel you possess?
- What strengths in Wren do you find that could become weaknesses if not used properly?
- What flaws did Wren have? How do you think they may have thwarted his success?
- Of the skills identified with Wren, which are opportunities for you?
- Do you feel Wren would be successful today?
- What challenges do you feel Wren would face today?

LEADERSHIP

CHAPTER ONE

The Leadership of Christopher Wren

IN MANY WAYS, CHRISTOPHER WREN may have been an ideal leader. He appears to be a balanced leader in that one could make an argument that he was both left and right brained. Wren was an architect, an engineer and an astronomer, all professions that would have required strong analytical skills for success. He was a scientist, providing many of the great advances in brain surgery and discovering the importance of antiseptic agents. Wren was an inventor, designing military devices as well as machines to lift water. But history suggests that he had many right brain tendencies as well. His early interest in art, his love of drawing and the building of several anatomical models for Dr. Thomas Willis are clear indicators of strong right brain tendencies. Additionally, he was a college professor, extremely modest in not seeking credit for most of his work, and a founding member of the Royal Society of London. Wren was perhaps a role model in not letting one's profession or comfort level box us in, preventing both individual and organizational effectiveness.

Christopher Wren may have been one of the first and best examples of MBWA—Management By Walking Around. Imagine Wren at his drafting table looking out over the construction area, grabbing his hard hat, and visiting with those who were bringing to fruition his architectural work. Imagine the reaction of the workers as Wren visited with each employee. It might have gone something like this: "You know, Wren is the only architect that has ever gotten out from behind his drafting table and spent time with us." Or maybe something like this: "He always asks about my children, he remembers my name, too."

Wren clearly understood and appreciated the difference between management and leadership. Wren was an effective manager, as evidenced by the fact that St. Paul's Cathedral is still standing today. There were deadlines and budgets to meet, quality control measures that had to be in place, employees and contractors to be supervised, and regular updates to the City of London—all very important things that managers do. But management is only one component of the equation; managers have to lead as well. Leaders have to ensure that employees see the Cathedral and not just go through the motions, viewing themselves as simply "laying bricks." Leaders have to communicate the mission and vision of the organization. They have to build teams and create a culture for peak performance.

In Clint Swindall's book, *Engaged Leadership*, he opines the answer to turning disengaged employees, the "Bricklayers," into engaged employees is through "Engaged Leadership." He states an employee is engaged or disengaged based on the culture of the organization, and that leaders must build a culture to overcome employee disengagement. He suggests three primary areas that all leaders must master in order to inspire and engage employees:

(1) Directional leadership, which builds consensus for the vision.

(2) Motivational leadership, which inspires others to pursue the vision.

(3) Organizational leadership, which develops the team to realize the vision.

Christopher Wren didn't seem to be a flashy or flamboyant leader, the kind we might think of when envisioning power brokers of his time. In fact, research suggests today's great leaders may not fit that profile either. In his bestselling book, *Good to Great,* Jim Collins studied companies that made the dramatic leap from simply "good" companies to "great" companies. Collins tracked 11 Fortune 500 companies over a five-year period and coined the term "Level 5 Leader" for leaders who blend extreme personal humility with intense professional will. Level 5 leaders channel their ego needs away from themselves and into the larger goal of building a great company. It's not that Level 5 leaders have no ego or self-interest. Collins suggests they are incredibly ambitious, but their ambition is first and foremost for the institution—for the Cathedral, not themselves.

Questions for Consideration

- What leadership qualities of Christopher Wren do you find most intriguing? Why?
- How do you feel Wren would fare as a modern-day leader?
- What type of culture do you think Wren would create today?
- What type of CEO would you think Wren would be?
- What type of leadership (directional, motivational, or organizational) do you feel Wren probably did the best? The worst?
- Of the three, which is most natural to you? Which is the least natural? Why?

- Where do you fall in Jim Collins' Level 5 hierarchy?

  ➢ **Level 1:** Highly Capable Individual: makes productive contributions through talent, knowledge, skills, and good work habits.

  ➢ **Level 2:** Contributing Team Member: Contributes individual capabilities to the achievement of group objectives and works effectively with others in a group setting.

  ➢ **Level 3:** Competent Manager: Organizes people and resources toward the effective and efficient pursuit of predetermined objectives.

  ➢ **Level 4:** Effective Leader: Catalyzes commitment to and vigorous pursuit of a clear and compelling vision, stimulating higher performance standards.

  ➢ **Level 5:** Level 5 Executive: Builds enduring greatness through a paradoxical blend of personal humility and professional will.

- Where do your direct reports fall in Jim Collins's Level 5 hierarchy? Your peers? Your boss?

CHAPTER TWO

Leadership That Insures
the Cathedral Gets Built

Dave Tatman

IT SHOULD BE ABUNDANTLY CLEAR by now that Cathedrals simply do not just happen. Many things go into the building of any Cathedral, but, at its heart, superior leadership skills must be present in a majority of the builders. Having been a lifelong student of leadership, I fundamentally believe that all of us have inherent leadership qualities. I don't buy into the notion of a "Born Leader" any more than I buy into the notion of a "Born Artist" or a "Born Athlete." We, as human beings, certainly have tendencies toward these things, but I believe that artists, athletes, or leaders are simply people who have taken their God-given gifts and honed them to a very high level by study, by practice, by training, and by a collective set of experiences.

It is important to first make the distinction between leadership and management. They are two related, yet different, things. The distinctions between the two have been the subject of work done by countless researchers and authors. I would submit that one of the simplest definitions was offered by noted author Warren Bennis, who is known as the "father of modern management." Bennis said, "Managers do things right, leaders do the right thing."

Understanding the contrasts between the two is vital, yet a common mistake is to confuse management with leadership. Distinguishing between the two is important to help us understand how we often neglect leadership at the expense of management.

- Leaders focus on people. Managers focus on things.
- Leaders deal with effectiveness. Managers worry about efficiency.
- Leaders study release and empowerment. Managers seek control.
- Leaders look for purpose. Managers seek methods.
- Leaders seek discernment. Managers chase measurement.
- A manager says, "Go!" A leader says, "Let's go!"

Both management and leadership are important organizational skills, but the question we must ask ourselves is this: Are we spending enough time leading? And while the distinctions between leadership and management are clear, we cannot be led to believe that one is more important than the other. We cannot choose between leadership OR management. We must choose leadership AND management. And while all organizations require both, our natural tendency is to default to managing and neglect leading. We cannot forget our responsibility to lead. In fact, Stephen Covey and many others have suggested that most modern day organizations are over-managed and under-led.

360 Degrees of Leadership

What exactly is the 360 degrees of leadership? Leadership in a circle? Leadership to all of your subordinates? Leadership that leaves no one out? No, none of the above. Leadership is much more than the view from the top down. When we typically think about the term "Leadership," our traditional paradigm revolves around people who are elected, appointed, or promoted to positions of leadership OVER others. While that is a very real leadership opportunity, leadership is much more than that. When properly integrated, 360 degree leadership allows us to avoid common pitfalls encountered by most leaders.

So a common question is, "How do I apply leadership principles if I'm not the boss?" It's a valid question and one that John Maxwell, Christian author, speaker and pastor, addresses in many of his more than 60 books primarily focused on leadership. In his best seller, *The 360 Degree Leader*, Maxwell asserts that we don't have to be THE leader to make a significant impact in our organization. Good leaders are not only capable of leading their followers; they are adept at leading superiors and peers. 360 degree leaders can lead effectively, regardless of their position in an organization. By applying these principles, we can expand our influence, be a more valuable team member and most importantly, ensure our Cathedrals get built!

360 degrees of leadership can best be explained by using the mental image of a vertical compass. The most effective leaders lead in four directions. They lead *South*—which is the traditional paradigm of leading others. They lead *East* and *West*, which is the opportunity to influence the actions of their peers through their own behaviors. They lead *North*, commonly referred to as "Leading Up." In this direction, their leadership role is to positively influence the leadership style of their superiors by actions and behaviors. And finally they lead inwardly by controlling their actions, words, and behaviors in an effort to provide a positive role model for everyone with whom they come in contact.

Leading South

Leading others (or Leading South) is the most traditional view of leadership, and the focus of most leadership writings and materials. People want to be led, but they want to be led in a way that instills confidence and a commitment to success. The job of a leader is to give people HOPE. One of the crucial enablers to leading others is the responsibility to clearly outline the vision and to consistently remind the team of its progress towards that vision.

In avoiding the "Yogi Berra" style of leadership—who said, "I don't know where we're headed, but we're making good progress"—it must be a leader's fundamental responsibility to ensure that everyone knows the Main Thing. That is, what we are we here for? What are the goals of the enterprise? How will we know when we are successful? What will keep us on the path to that success?

People want and need to know they are part of something larger and greater than just themselves. Way too often, leaders fail to recognize their responsibility to inspire others in the mission and objectives of the organization. People often feel their contributions don't really matter and they fall into "The Rut of the Rat Race." The problem with the rat race is that even if we win it, we're still rats!

If we are to be leaders, our job is to inspire others to greatness. They must feel a part of something greater than that which they could achieve on their own. People follow people, not positions. Our ability to inspire others is a key enabler to our leadership success. One of the most powerful tools in leading others is the Power of Perpetual Optimism.

An organization will assume the mood of its leader. If we demonstrate an upbeat, positive, can-do kind of attitude, it will be reflected back to us by our team. General Colin Powell in *A Leadership Primer*, says that "Perpetual Optimism is a Force Multiplier." The ripple effect of a leader's enthusiasm and optimism is an awesome thing. Unfortunately, so is the impact of cynicism and pessimism. Leaders who whine and blame others engender those same behaviors among their colleagues. I am not talking about stoically accepting organizational stupidity and performance incompetence with a "What, me worry?" smile. I am talking about a gung-ho attitude that says, "We CAN change things here, we CAN achieve awesome goals, we CAN be the best." Spare me the grim litany of the realist; give me the unrealistic aspirations of the optimist any day!

Leading East and West

The East and West directions of our leadership compass—or leading across and among our peers and colleagues—is an interesting leadership challenge. Think of a time where you when part of a team where others on the team were simply not pulling their weight. While we generally cannot control the actions and behaviors of others, we do have a powerful way to influence our peers, and that is through our words, actions, and behaviors. In these situations, no one has positional power and we find ourselves in a balanced game. The key to lateral leadership lies in an attitude of service above self. We must act and behave in such a way that others recognize we are in this together. Examine your heart and motives in these times, and ensure you are acting in a way that places team success ahead of personal success. Others will recognize this and respond favorably.

To further accelerate growth of our peer team, our ability to admit and acknowledge our strengths and weaknesses in the company of our colleagues creates an environment of trust that will pave the way for success. Our role as lateral leaders is to be vulnerable. Can we admit that others just might be smarter, better, stronger, or more skilled at certain things than we are? Doing so opens the door to trusting one another and creates a real, open, honest, and trusting setting where success is inevitable. It also opens up a powerful spirit of accountability that is crucial to the team's accomplishment. When we trust one another, we are far more likely to engage in the tough discussions that are required to achieve peer-to-peer accountability. Our actions as lateral leaders must epitomize our belief that the team is THE highest priority.

Leading North

We are called as leaders to lead up, or North, as well. We often don't think of this, but the people to whom you report need your leadership as well. We must learn to lead up. But let us be clear here: Leading Up is NOT sucking up!! There are those in leadership positions who do not like to be told bad news. They seek to surround themselves with "Yes-People." If you are a Yes-Man with your boss, one of you is redundant! Which one? Your call...

Since leading up is probably the least practiced skill, here are some tips that may help in this matter:

- Do your job. Demonstrate competency. Exceed expectations. There is no substitute for simply doing good work. Every leader appreciates this in his or her subordinate. Never, ever, take this for granted. Do the things that are expected of you and exceed those expectations. Every day. No excuses.

- Establish a relationship with your boss on a personal level. I don't mean that you need to be social friends or play golf together. I am saying get to know your boss in ways that are perhaps not typical. What are the names of her children? Where did he grow up? What is her favorite food or restaurant? How does he spend his spare time? Doing so will open up a whole new dimension to your supervisor-subordinate relationship. This will likely allow you latitude in influencing your boss's style. Influence and relationship are inseparably linked.

- Discover your boss's style. For instance, what is the best time of their day or the best place to have those difficult discussions that will influence their behaviors? Moreover, determine how they want to be influenced. Do you simply offer your observations of specific leadership circumstances, or does he or she prefer a more direct environment of constructive feedback?

When you Lead Up, it is your responsibility to use your talents and skills to help the overall organization achieve its objectives. Leading Up is not an effort to get your personal accomplishments recognized or some other self-serving agenda. It is, and always must be, about the team. Being able to influence the leadership behavior of your superiors by Leading North is a powerful enabler to overall organizational success.

Self-Leadership

The single biggest factor, in my judgment, separating good leaders from great leaders lies in this area of Self-Leadership. Controlling our own attitudes and behaviors requires discipline. It is frequently easier, yet wrong, to default to our natural tendency of Leading Down, when we should be looking to Leading Within.

Make it a habit to reflect on your Self Leadership by frequently asking yourself these questions:

- Is my vision clear?
- Is my calling sure?
- Is my passion burning hot?
- Is my pace sustainable?
- Are my character and integrity fully intact?
- Is my pride subdued?
- Are my fears at bay?
- Are my eyes and ears open to the words and actions of others?

The white-hot crucible of leadership opportunity is that others are constantly watching you. Your words, your actions, and your behaviors are all contributors to the way in which others will respond, whether they are your subordinates, your peers, or your supervisor. We cannot control others; we can only control ourselves. We must constantly work on developing the skills of self-awareness and self-leadership to truly make the leap to becoming a great leader.

The 360 Degrees of Leadership: Lead Down, Lead Across, Lead

Up, and Lead Within. All are critical to our success as leaders and key differentiators in our future. Never stop learning. All of us have innate leadership skills. Great leaders are the ones who nourish and develop these skills.

In my mind, there are three fundamental leadership principles that should guide us as we use the 360 Degrees of Leadership to build our Cathedrals:

1. People do not care how much you know until they know how much you care.

2. People don't have to have their own way; they just need to know that their own way has been considered.

3. People can handle bad news—what they cannot handle is anything less than the truth.

Questions for Consideration

- Think about your leadership skills. Which ones are more natural and which ones are more learned? Explain.

- How do you feel about leaders being born or created? Explain.

- What and where do you feel are the best training grounds for leadership?

- Describe the difference between management and leadership.

- Can a person be in management and not be a leader? Why or why not?

- Can a person be a leader and not be in management? Why or why not?
- Which one are you most comfortable with and why?
- Which one do you feel is the most important?
- Of the 360 Degrees of Leadership, which one do you feel you embrace the most and why?
- Of the 360 Degrees of Leadership, which do you feel is the most important?
- Which of the 360 Degrees of Leadership do you consider the most challenging for you?
- What are the challenges and limitations of each, and how do they align with your current leadership skill set?
- What is your favorite leadership model?

CHAPTER THREE

"Any nation that does not honor its heroes will not endure."

—Abraham Lincoln

Be-Know-Do

I FIRST HEARD OF General Carmen Cavezza (Ret.) from a friend of mine in Columbus, Georgia. Like General Dan Cherry, who you will read about later, General Cavezza continues to build Cathedrals when most folks who have achieved what they have are looking to slow down. General Cavezza retired from the United States Army, where he was the Base Commander at Fort Benning, the nation's largest Army base. General Cavezza is the current Chair of the Columbus, Georgia Chamber of Commerce, interim Chair of the United States Army Infantry Museum, Executive Director of the Cunningham Leadership Center at Columbus State University, and former City Manager for Columbus, Georgia. My friend had just heard the retired General speak to a group of businesspeople and quickly emailed me a summary of his points:

- Never depend on the first report, especially if it's an emotional issue.

- Be yourself—the best leader you can be is you.

- Establish and live your values.

43

- If you have good people, get out of their way and let them be good.

- Look for the pony in the barn and not just the poop on the floor.

- Be an optimist.

- Be a good listener—James 1:19 says, "Be swift to hear, slow to speak, slow to wrath."

- Be patient—what looks bad at the end of the day will look better the next morning.

- Don't accept problems from people without hearing their suggested solution.

- Always strive to be better—when you die, there's always unused space in your brain.

- When you're satisfied, you're ineffective.

I couldn't wait to meet General Cavezza, and as I waited in the conference room I anticipated his perspective on leadership. Would he reference Peter Drucker or would he cite the military leadership of Generals Patton, Schwarzkopf, or Powell? Would he be a Blanchard follower or a Covey follower? General Cavezza was indeed an impressive man, yet his presence and his character made me feel comfortable and at ease. His response, simple yet powerful, was very much like his demeanor: "Greg, I can sum up my general perspective on leadership in three simple words: BE, KNOW, DO."

Wondering what leadership book he must have read that I had obviously overlooked in my 20 plus years of studying the subject, I asked, "Be, Know, Do"?

His response, "BE, KNOW, DO, *Army Leadership Field Manual 22-100*, which lays out the framework that applies to all Army leaders—officer and NCO, military and civilian, active and reserve. At the core of our leadership doctrine are the same Army values embedded in our force: loyalty, duty, respect, selfless service, honor, integrity and personal courage."

General Cavezza continued, "The Army does two things every day: It trains soldiers and develops leaders. When leadership in business breaks down, employees become disengaged, the culture deteriorates and profits can spiral out of control. When leadership in our Armed Forces breaks down, people die." Leadership in business is important; leadership in the Army is essential!

General Cavezza defined leadership as influencing people by providing purpose, direction, and motivation while operating to accomplish the mission and improving the organization. "In short, leadership in the Army transforms human potential into effective performance," said Cavezza.

That small conference room was quickly transformed into a classroom as the professor continued the lecture that would change my entire perspective on leadership. General Cavezza said that we demonstrate character through our behavior and one of the key responsibilities of a leader is to teach values to subordinates. Therefore, the General explained, Army leadership begins with what the leader must BE, with the values and attributes that shape a leader's character.

He described the Army values as:

- *Loyalty*: Bearing true faith and allegiance to the U.S. Constitution, the Army, the unit, and other soldiers.
- *Duty*: Fulfilling all obligations.
- *Respect*: Treating people as they should be treated.
- *Selfless service*: Putting the welfare of the nation, the Army, and subordinates before one's own.
- *Honor*: Living up to all the Army values.
- *Integrity*: Doing what's right—legally and morally.

- *Personal courage*: Facing fear, danger, or adversity (physical or moral).

Skills are those things people KNOW how to do, such as competence from the technical side of a job and the people skills required for leadership. Leaders must have a high level of knowledge and mastery of four basic skills:

- *Interpersonal skills*: coaching, teaching, counseling, motivating and empowering others, as well as building teams.

- *Conceptual skills*: the ability to think creatively and to reason analytically, critically, and ethically which are the basis of sound judgment.

- *Technical skills*: job-related abilities that are necessary to accomplish the task at hand.

- *Tactical skills*: in the Army, those skills required to deploy units into combat.

And while character and knowledge are necessary, leaders must apply what they know; they must act and DO what they have learned is effective. Successful leaders build teams, execute plans, and lead change in their organizations. In the Army's language, the three areas that a leader must DO are:

- *Influence*: using interpersonal skills to lead others toward a goal, communicating clearly, motivating others and recognizing achievement.

- *Operate*: developing and executing plans, managing resources, identifying strengths and weaknesses.

- *Improve*: good leaders strive to leave the organization in better shape than they found it. They believe in life-long learning, always seeking self-improvement, and organizational growth and development. Good leaders are also change agents.

At the end of my time with General Cavezza, I was speech-less. I have attended hundreds of seminars, listened to hours and hours of lectures, read a room full of books, and yet never thought of spending time with the epitome of a leader: a military officer. And sadly, since the end of the draft and the establishment of the all-volunteer force in 1973, fewer and fewer civilians are being exposed to the Army, its leadership and its training. And ironi-cally, many of us live only a short distance from a military base, where numerous opportunities to learn from the nation's most committed team of soldiers and the most effective leaders in the world wait for us. All we need to do is simply call the public in-formation officer and arrange a tour and a briefing from the Base Commander and his leadership team.

Questions for Consideration

- What are your general thoughts about military leadership?
- What are your thoughts about the perceived "tough love" leadership approach in the military?
- How do you think military leadership has evolved over the years?
- What are the major challenges of military lead-ership today?
- What can we learn from military leadership?
- How can civilian leadership capitalize on mili-tary leadership? Would you consider visiting a local military base? What are the similari-ties between civilian leadership and military leadership?

- What could the military learn from the private sector?

- What military leadership skills resonate with your plans to become a Cathedral Builder?

THE FIRE

"When you walk through fire you shall not be burned, and the flame shall not consume you."

—Isaiah 43:2

CHAPTER FOUR

The Great Fire of 1666

THE GREAT FIRE OF 1666 BEGAN early on the morning of September 2nd at a London bakery. The fire spread extremely fast, as most homes and buildings were made of a very flammable wood-pitch combination and were built dangerously close to one another. Hay piles, warehouses filled with coal, wood and alcohol fed the already disastrous fire. And while the loss of life was amazingly low (less than 20), the loss of property was astronomical. 430 acres, 13,000 homes and 89 churches were totally destroyed, leaving thousands homeless and financially ruined.

While the fire of 1666 was indeed a catastrophic event, there were many positives that resulted from a devastated London. The plague, which had ravaged London for many years, was greatly diminished due to the mass death of disease carrying rats and fleas. The mass destruction gave city leaders an opportunity to rebuild London to be a great city. Streets were widened, buildings were rebuilt with less flammable brick and regulations were strengthened. Improvements to sanitation, overcrowding and communication within the city were also made. Additionally, firefighting techniques and strategies were greatly enhanced.

The city that had burned was a medieval one; the London that emerged from its ruins was a modern one. The process of rebuilding began quickly, with over 7000 new buildings by 1671. London made a powerful statement to the rest of the world as the King initiated several grand structures demonstrating that the city was indeed back in business. While the Royal Exchange and a new Customs House arguably had vital economic functions, many structures were perceived to be pure symbolism. London quickly became the model for modern design, with some of America's greatest cities being influenced by the work of Christopher Wren.

ST. PAUL'S CATHEDRAL

While Wren was responsible for over 50 churches, his most famous work was clearly St. Paul's Cathedral. Since World War II, St. Paul's Cathedral has been Britain's symbol of resistance. Despite 57 nights of bombing, the Nazis failed to destroy the Cathedral, thanks to St. Paul's volunteer fire watchman, who manned the 365-foot dome. London's first known church dedicated to St. Paul was built on the current site in the year 604. Made of wood, it burned down in 675, and Viking invaders destroyed a subsequent church in 962. The third church was built of stone. Following another fire in 1087, it was rebuilt as a much larger cathedral, with walls of stone and a wooden roof completed in 1300. In 1666, Wren's plans to restore the building had just been accepted when the Great Fire of London burned the old cathedral to the ground.

Questions for Consideration

- How would the response to the fire of 1666 be different today?

- In what ways have you seen others deal with devastation?

- What character traits are important in rebuilding from the "ashes of difficult life circumstances"?

- What "fires" have you had in your life?

- How did you respond?

- Did you respond as you wish you would have responded?

- St. Paul's Cathedral became Britain's symbol for resistance. What is yours?

- Rats and fleas were eradicated after the fire of 1666, allowing London to rebuild. What "rats and fleas" do you need to eradicate?"

- What "fires" has your organization had?

- Were there positives that came out of the "fires" in your organization?

AFTER THE FIRE: The Rebuilding Begins

CHAPTER FIVE

All Stressed Up and No Place to Go
Skip Wirth

"ALL STRESSED UP AND NO PLACE TO GO" repre-
sents a blueprint for building or rebuilding one of the most important "Cathedrals,"....YOU, after the "personal fires" in your
life. For over 36 years, stress, its effects on the body and life management skills for mediating the harmful effects of chronic stress,
has been my passion, my personal "Cathedral." Throughout the
years, I have spoken to well over 1000 audiences on some form
of this topic, and for good reason. Stress is now recognized as
the number-one killer. This is not the world according to Skip;
this comes from the American Medical Association. In fact, the
American Institute of Stress estimates that 90 percent of all visits
to doctors are for stress-related disorders. How can this be? Have
you ever picked up your newspaper and read a headline stating,
"Another Person Killed by Stress"? Not likely. Stress is a killer by
proxy and is behind the five leading causes of death in America.

Several weeks following September 11, 2001, I was invited to
be the guest speaker for a Chamber of Commerce. I eagerly accepted the offer, but my thoughts quickly turned to, "What can I
say to this group that will help to lift their spirits, give them hope,
and help them to reclaim those parts of theirs lives that have them
spinning out of control?" America was still hurting; my audience
was still hurting. The memories of that horrible day still haunted

them. My speech, "All Stressed Up and No Place to Go," was written precisely for this occasion. In essence, it is an overview of seven characteristics of stress resistance, or strategies to help "After the Fire." Much credit goes to Dr. Raymond B. Flannery, Jr. who authored the book, *Becoming Stress Resistant,* a must read!

We all know people who just seem to glide through life. Even though they encounter difficult life circumstances, they always bounce back. What do they have that others don't? If they have it, can we have it also? How much of it do we need? Is it possible to incorporate what they do into our lives and become more like them? YES!

In studying these individuals, researchers such as Dr. Flannery, Dr. Herbert Benson and Hans Selye, among many others, have identified characteristics these people have in common that make them less vulnerable to the harmful effects of stress, characteristics that add years to your life and life to your years, building a better Cathedral.

The seven characteristics of stress resistant people or "those who come out of the fire" are as follows:

1. *Those who come out of the fire take personal control.* When confronted with a problem or stressor, these people take charge. They take self-initiated, self-directed problem solving strategies to resolve the problem. They don't roll over and wait for others to come to their rescue. They are empowered, not overpowered. They know what personal resources are available to them and they bring them to bear. After the great fire of 1666, or more recently, the horror of 9/11, feelings of being out of control were pervasive. However, in both instances, those feelings were replaced with planned, organized and self-directed strategies to rebuild their lives.

2. *Those who come out of the fire are task involved.* All of us need a reason to live. A purpose in life. A task that we are personally or existentially committed to. Examples of task involvement include

our families, jobs, church activities, hobbies, volunteer projects, and our pets. We need to feel like we matter, that we make a difference. We know it as self-esteem. We strive to become valued partners in our life's journey. Have you noticed that when a person retires from work but fails to fill that once occupied space with something meaningful, they often wither and die? Boredom is a very powerful, negative life force and is best avoided. The German philosopher Friedrich Nietzsche wrote, "A person with a 'why' to live for can bear most any 'how.'" Keep building those Cathedrals!

3. *Those who come out of the fire seek social support.* We need one another, and this need is biologically rooted. You may tell yourself, "If it weren't for all of these people, I would feel more sane." Quite the opposite is true. Research shows that people with few or no close contacts die at higher rates for every major cause of death. Recently, chronic loneliness was risk-equated to a one-pack-per-day smoking habit. If you are a lonely smoker, you are in deep doo! Just for a moment, reflect on all the helpful social exchanges in your life: love, affection, trust, respect, support, empathy, nurturing, dignity, appreciation, listening, caring and bonding, just to name a handful. We need one another! We always have, before and especially, after the fire.

4. *Those who come out of the fire make wise lifestyle choices.* This is where the rubber meets the road. Mark Twain wrote, "The only way to keep your health is to eat what you don't want, drink what you do not like, and do what you'd rather not." Unfortunately, far too many Americans subscribe to that notion. In 2001, the Centers for Disease Control (CDC) reported that only one-fourth of American adults exercised enough in the 1990s. Only 25.4 % of adults met government recommendations for physical activity. Nearly 30 % reported no physical activity at all (except for blinking and clicking). The CDC recommends 30 minutes of moderate exercise, like walking, five times a week, or 20 minutes of vigorous exercise such as running, cycling, rowing or swimming, three times a week. The 30-minute requirement can be broken into

chunks as small as 10 minutes with everyday activities such as gardening. Walking may be the perfect exercise. "Regular physical activity such as walking is probably as close to a magic bullet as we will come in modern medicine," said Dr. JoAnn Manson, Chief of Preventative Medicine at Harvard's Brigham and Women's Hospital. "If everyone in the U.S. were to walk briskly 30 minutes a day, we could cut the incidence of many chronic diseases 30% to 40%." Modifications in lifestyle could prevent or delay 75% of illness and disease. This is startling! What comprises the remaining 25%? Genetics, for which you have no control over, and environment, for which you have very little control over. That 75% modification in lifestyle is a large, powerful stick for which you have complete control! Just for clarity, lifestyle encompasses your diet, exercise, stress management, sleep, safety (do you wear seat belts?), substance use/abuse (smoking, excessive alcohol, drug abuse), as well as other lifestyle factors. When you make wise lifestyle choices, your Cathedral becomes your "Fortress."

5. *Those who come out of the fire have a sense of humor.* When I was young, I remember hearing on a television variety show, "Laughter is the best medicine." I remember thinking that sounded great, but how do they know that? Do doctors prescribe laughter for their patients? Sure, laughter feels good like a warm blanket, but the best medicine? In recent years, a great deal of scientific evidence supports that assertion. Humor and laughter stimulate the immune system, lowers blood pressure, increases endorphin levels (the hormone that makes you feel good), decreases stress, helps oxygen to be utilized more efficiently, and helps to control pain. Too bad we can't put humor in a pill form and bottle it! Researchers discovered that on average, toddlers laugh 400 times a day. Adults laugh only 15 times a day. My first impression, "What a rip-off! What price am I paying by giving up 385 laughs a day?" Actually, my laughing habits are more like the toddlers. Researchers also found that anger (the opposite of happiness) triples mortality rates, and that whining, which is anger through a smaller opening, has similar consequences. While

building your Cathedral, perhaps you might consider whistling while you work.

6. *Those who come out of the fire espouse religious values and have an ethical regard for others.* This probably comes as no surprise to most of you, even in our "get ahead at any cost," competitive environment. All of the great religions of the world say the same thing: love your neighbor. You remember the Golden Rule— do unto others. Dust it off because it still applies in a deep and visceral way. Studies show that religious people tend to live healthier lives. "They are less likely to smoke, to drink, to drink and drive," says Harold Koenig, M.D., Associate Professor of Medicine at Duke. In fact, people who pray tend to get sick less often, as separate studies at Duke, Dartmouth and Yale Universities reveal. Some statistics from these studies:

- Hospitalized people who never attended church have an average stay of three times longer than people who attended regularly.
- Heart patients were 14 times more likely to die following surgery if they did not participate in a religion.
- Elderly people who never or rarely attended church had a stroke rate double that of people who attended regularly.
- In Israel, religious people had a 40% lower death rate from cardiovascular disease and cancer.

Also, says Koenig, "People who are more religious tend to become depressed less often. And when they do become depressed, they recover quickly from depression. That has consequences for their physical health and the quality of their lives." What goes on in our personal Cathedrals is powerful medicine indeed!

7. *Those who come out of the fire are optimistic.* I am fortunate because I inherited this one from my mother. Throughout my youth and adulthood, she was the epitome of optimism—light, cheery, funny, and encouraging. She was one of life's cheerleaders. Optimism, a close cousin to happiness, protects the heart and lungs, boosts the immune system, reinforces self-esteem and helps reduce long-term stress. Studies now prove that happy people are "more likely to get and stay married, have friends and participate in organizations," says Sonja Lyubomitsky from the University of California at Riverside. "They are more likely to pursue goals, be more energetic, more likely to be hired and be less likely to be fired."

"Optimism is a frame for how you view the world and happiness is an emotion," explains Harvard University's Laura Kubzanksy. Just 10% of happiness comes from individual circumstances, 50% from genetic inheritance and 40% is uncharted. Do you know how to tell the difference between an optimist and a pessimist? An optimist wakes up in the morning and proclaims, "God, it's a good morning!" A pessimist wakes up in the morning and grunts, "Good God, its morning!" Same morning—different view. After the fire, the third bricklayer knew all along that both London and St. Paul's Cathedral would be rebuilt better than ever.

These seven characteristics are not unlike ingredients to a wonderful recipe. Incorporate these ingredients into your life and something wonderful transforms—YOU! In order to make these ingredients easier to remember, I have repackaged them into "Skipisms" that I call "The Seven F's":

- Faith
- Family
- Friends
- Food
- Fun
- Fitness
- Focus

What a recipe for life! Bon Appetit!

"For I know the plans I have for you. They are plans for good and not evil, to give you a future and a hope."

—Jeremiah 29:11

Questions for Consideration

- Do you consider "YOU" as a Cathedral? If so, how? If not, why?

- What impact do you think your Cathedral presence is having among those around you?

- Out of the seven characteristics, which one(s) do you do a pretty good job with? Which one(s) do you need to work on?

- What characteristics would you add to Skip Wirth's list?

- Consider organizations that have come out of "fire." What characteristics were evident? What role did leadership play?

CHAPTER SIX

After the Devastation; After the Fire:
A journey to believing that God is still good
even when bad things happen
Candice Ashburn

IT WAS JUNE 4, 2007, and a Monday that started just like any other day in the life of a cardiac surgery resident and his wife—awakened by a beeper.

4:00 AM David returned the page and the conversation ensued that he would fly from Ann Arbor to Milwaukee to retrieve organs for a transplant.

10:00 AM He called to tell me he was taking off and would call me again before their departure from Milwaukee. That was our routine when he flew.

4:00 PM Organ procurement complete. Ready to return the lungs to the recipient waiting on the operating table at the University of Michigan Medical Center in Ann Arbor.

4:52 PM David called me on my cell phone. No answer. We were in ballet. I left my phone in the car.

4:53 PM David called me at the house. No answer. He never left messages. I believe he was calling me to tell me he was taking off and would be home soon. Little did I know, and little did he know, I believe, that he indeed would be Home in a matter of minutes.

5:08 PM The Cessna citation crashed almost immediately after take-off. David and 5 other men were on board.

Search and Rescue eventually turned into Search and Recovery, which lasted an inordinate amount of time—weeks and weeks. The weather did not cooperate which made searching the waters difficult, if not impossible. Though not all of the remains were found, official Search and Recovery was concluded by the end of June.

Just a couple of weeks before the accident, David and I happened to have had a conversation about how we wanted our funerals to be—and not be, should the Lord take us Home. We both concurred, no open casket, please. Neither of us wanted anyone to be focused on the physical remains, because that was not what was "remaining" anyway. We both confirmed to one another that we wanted a "celebration of life-lived and eternal." So, not having a body was not an emotional event for me. The process itself was very emotional. The fact was not. I never thought too much about not having his body under the circumstances of his death. I was either in too much shock to think about it or, it was God's grace. I think it was both. But there was one thing I asked to have back.

In July, I was at my sister's house in Huntsville when I got a phone call about midnight with some "good news" and some "bad news." The bad news was that a large portion of human remains had been found by several sailors on Lake Michigan long after the official Search and Recovery had ended. The good news was that it was identified as David's—and that was good because it provided the surprising answer to my prayer.

What I had previously asked God to give me back was David's wedding band . . . which, at the time, would have been nothing short of a miracle since I had no idea what would be found or left after such a crash. It was equivalent to finding a needle in a haystack. For graphic reasons that I won't describe, the ring was the only way that they knew the corpse was David's. His ring had both of our initials engraved in it.

It reminded me of the scripture in Isaiah 49:16 that says,

"See I have engraved you on the palm of my hands; your walls are ever before me."

Just as David's ring had his initials engraved on it which identified him under unrecognizable conditions, I knew God had my name engraved on His palms and that meant I would never be lost, abandoned, or unaccounted for in this life that was unimaginably unrecognizable to me.

I'm not sure what is more amazing . . . that God would return David's ring to me under these circumstances or the mere fact that my sweet David actually had his ring on so soon after leaving the OR. It was quite unusual that surgeons would wear a wedding band at all. They have to take it off to scrub in, and the likelihood of losing it by taking it on and off was great. But David insisted on wearing his. He thought it was important. So for almost 10 years, he would wear his ring every day and when he took it off to operate, he would tie it to his scrub pant draw string. Then afterwards, put it back on. He never lost it. And so he did that day, too. He wasn't a perfect husband, nor was I a perfect wife. But we were committed to starting over every day in this thing called marriage . . . that's part of my pain in the loss of our marriage. We had lived the good, the bad, and the ugly—and continued to choose covenant and commitment over comfort and conceit.

His ring was returned to me . . . in a Fed Ex box along with the other personal articles of his that were recovered at the crash site: his stethoscope, his wallet contents, and his lab coat. What is one to expect of the belongings of their loved one which have survived the elements of a plane crash? Would his once stark white lab coat be tattered, torn, charred or burned? Or would it have been cleaned before being returned?

"What am I supposed to do with these things? How can I open the box that holds all of what was left of him, Lord? The man who courted me, pursued me, whom You gave me to have and to hold forever . . . has now been reduced to this box. "

Well . . . that specific answer is another story for another day. But God did whisper sweetly that He did not intend for the contents in the box to haunt me but to help me remember that He (God) hears every cry of my heart and does not miss a beat (the stethoscope); that He would always take care of me physically (the physician's lab coat); and that He would be the husband that I had no more (his wedding ring).

The "Fed Ex" box sits unopened on the same shelf next to David's ashes that were just recently mailed to me in a US Postal Service box.

The postman walks up to my front door, "I've got something for you, mam."

If he only knew. Great.

Have you ever held out your hands to receive a box and it was a lot lighter than you thought it was going to be? I don't know what I was expecting, but I held out my hands to receive the box of ashes, and it was so much heavier than I anticipated that I almost dropped it. It was then that my body went into shock almost like it did the night that I received the news of David's crash. My hands and arms were numb and tingling, and I found myself asking, yet again, "What am I to do with this, Lord?"

And then another whisper from God.

"I will give you beauty for ashes . . . right here at this door."

> *To provide for those who grieve . . .*
>
> *to bestow on them a crown of beauty instead of ashes . . .*
>
> *gladness instead of mourning. . .*
>
> *praise instead of despair . . .*

for the display of HIS splendor . . .

restore the places long devastated . . .

they will inherit a double portion . . . and everlasting joy will be theirs.

—Isaiah 61:3-7

The whispers of God don't change that I was widowed at 34, left with a 4 year old, a 2 year old, and a 10 month old with Down syndrome.

It doesn't change the questions that I still ask myself sometimes:

"Did David really die?"

"Did he really die in a plane crash — trying to save someone else's life?"

"Did he really die just one year away from the end of the long ten year residency road?"

"Are my children really without a father?"

"Am I really going to have to explain all of this to them one day?"

And because the short answer to those questions is "yes," "I spend most of my time with my heart bowed to the One who has appointed this life for me…and He has been enough."

"I'm Building a Cathedral to The Almighty"

My response and deepest heart's desire to such circumstance has been to represent God well. My testimony is that our testimony is one of the things that will preserve our life in times of hardship, heartache and our personal fires (Acts 4:20). Even through some of life's greatest difficulties, there has never been another option for me except to trust God. "God is still good" were the words I uttered the night of David's crash. Even if they were spoken through tears and shock, that is what I believed then, and that is what I believe now. "God did not fall asleep on that June 4 day, nor did He step away from His throne and have to revert to plan B. God was in control of my ("well planned") life before June 4, 2007, and He is still in control."

I don't know of another god in the universe whose followers can proclaim that which followers of Christ can proclaim: that He is alive and well and reigns in the hearts of those who love Him… and practically speaking, that He is ever aware of the details of our days. I know that to be true as God has delivered me every single day since David's sudden and tragic death to this point in my journey. I am utterly amazed to look back and remember what God has enabled me to accomplish — practically, mentally, physically and spiritually. He truly is a God who delights in doing the impossible…(Luke 1:37 and Matthew 19:26)

I share God's amazing grace and love as I share my journey of love and life, disability and death. In a Christmas letter 5 months before David's death, referring to the news that our newborn had Down's syndrome, I wrote, "I have learned that God places us exactly where He wants us, to grow us and to share Him with the world! The blessings that have come from initially devastating news have been indescribable. He does make beauty from ashes."

My challenge is for you to recognize God's plan, see His glory, and experience the fullness of His grace in your own life and to join me in "Building a Cathedral to The Almighty."

Visit Candice Ashburn's Cathedral at
www.herpassionministries.com

Question for Consideration

- What can we learn from Candice Ashburn and her story?

Author's Note

Patty is my sister and I am honored that she agreed to share her story. I am very proud of her. She was the first of our family (on both my mother and father's side of the family) to attend college. She graduated and went to work for NASA and then the National Security Agency in Washington, DC. She then followed her passion, her Cathedral, and went to work for several Christian-based organizations. She indeed had a profound influence on me personally as well as professionally. In fact, I'm not sure I would have chosen to attend college had it not been for my sister. She has always been a person of faith, and I often wondered why God didn't talk to me like He did my sister. After years and years of questioning and frustration, I finally broke the code. She spent time with Him. She had a personal relationship with our Heavenly Father. She could always be found as a young child reading her Bible and studying His Word. But like all of us, she has experienced personal "fires." But just like London, she has weathered the storm and is doing well. In fact, how she dealt with devastation and the emotional roller coaster she went through during those times served as a role model of how I would deal with a similar devastation just months later. Perhaps most of the credit for helping my sister and me through the fires of our lives should go to our parents. They have always been there for us, and, unfortunately, taken on the pain we were feeling and experiencing. It has been said that a parent is only as happy as his or her unhappiest child. How true. So pick up the phone and call that sibling and let your brother or sister know how much you love them. Let that person know his or her positive influence on your life. And while you're at it, call your parents and thank them for their support and their love .

CHAPTER SEVEN

Faith to Move Mountains; Faith to Build Cathedrals

Patty Brightup

WHEN THE PEOPLE OF ENGLAND witnessed the mass destruction from the fire of 1666, they were obviously devastated. Everything they had worked so hard to build was destroyed in the fire. They must have surely felt like all their hard work and energy had been in vain. But at some point, after the grieving process, they probably asked, "What now?" And, as they envisioned the work and energy it would take to rebuild, they may have asked, "Why rebuild just to see it destroyed again?" We are no different. After we experience devastation in our lives, we often become so overwhelmed by our sorrows that we are discouraged and reluctant to rebuild.

But when we experience a loss, we need to know there is a God who heals all sorrows and takes tremendous joy in walking with us as we rebuild. We need strength *beyond* what we have in our moment of despair to get through our personal fires. God will give you that strength even during the times when you're questioning His will, His presence, His reasoning. Even when things aren't turning around quickly enough for you, do not despair. Believe that God is doing something on your behalf, even when you can't see it. Eventually, you will be able to look back and realize God had an amazing way that He worked all this out for you.

I have experienced several devastations that make this story very real to me. My marriage of 20 years suddenly came to an end. A house that we had just built on a beautiful farm had to be sold. The engine on my car went out which resulted in expenses and hardship. My children had medical issues after they were involved in an automobile accident. I had college expenses that I had no idea how I would pay. And then, as if the fire couldn't get any hotter, the smoke any more smothering, I was summoned to my manager's office one Friday afternoon. Fuel on the already blazing fire was the news that my job was being eliminated.

I must admit, there was a point that I thought, "Even God Himself must be against me!" I have believed in God all my life. Within moments after I uttered those words and was crying hard, I pulled myself together and I prayed this very powerful prayer. "God, I thank you for everything You are doing on my family's behalf, even that which I cannot see. Amen." I just had to believe God cared for what happened to me and my boys and that He heard my cry. I just had to believe that God was doing something for me that I couldn't see at that moment. I had to believe that one day I would look back and see how God worked it out for me. And, He did. Had it not been for my faith, I don't know how I would have made it through all my challenges, hardships and devastations.

You may have experienced more traumatic devastations than I and I am not trying to minimize your personal fires. But please believe and know that God will heal your sorrow and help restore all that you've lost. You can rebuild. There are Cathedrals out there that God intended for you to build—Cathedrals that need your expertise, your passion. We just have to believe that God will enable and equip us.

Just as the people of London felt like everything they had built had been in vain, I felt the very same way. I had poured my life, my time, my energy and my commitment into my marriage, my home and my career and it had so quickly been taken away. But once I realized that I was blessed with life itself, I began living in the goodness of God and my whole attitude and outlook changed. I started to realize that home is where you make it and that family is the most important part of our life.

After the devastation and after the smoke cleared, what remained was actually the most important, not what had gone up in smoke. My family, my faith, and my salvation were the most important things in my life. Getting through the devastating moments of your life is a painful process. Getting past the devastation is a process of both healing and restoration. What seems impossible will be very possible with God's help. Your hope will be what refuels your rebuilding, allowing you to envision something good and dream a plan for your future. Your setbacks and disappointments can't rob you of who you are. People lose jobs. Marriages fall apart. Cars get damaged. Houses blow away. Even our bodies will someday wear out and we will leave this earth. We will not be remembered for our career, our home or our stuff. We will be remembered by those people who were impacted by our life…by the Cathedrals that we build that live on forever.

Our lives are Cathedrals that glorify God and inspire others. During my devastation, I was responsible for my family, my Cathedrals that survived the devastation. All the decisions that I made were in the interest of preserving those Cathedrals. Naturally and importantly, I poured most of my time, energy and money into my family, often neglecting my own Cathedral. God, the Master Builder, went to work rebuilding my broken heart and spirit and with time and patience God helped me rebuild my Cathedral so that I might give Glory to Him through a restored life. But I had to ask Him. You have to ask Him.

The rebuilding is worth it! In fact, what we rebuild will have a greater purpose than it did before. Our lives will have more meaning and purpose than ever before. Our personal witness will be even stronger. Regardless of whether you're rebuilding what you lost or building something new, have the faith to move mountains in your life. Have the faith to build the Cathedrals.

Questions for Consideration

- What can we learn from Patty and her story?
- How does the stress we experience affect others?
- Are you there for your family members during the fires in their lives?
- Are you there for your friends and co-workers during the fires in their lives?
- Have you given your parents, family and friends the proper thanks and appreciation for all that they've done for you, especially during the fires in your life?

Send us your stories of how you've successfully come out of your personal fires at mycathedral@thecathedralinstitute.com

CATHEDRALS

CHAPTER EIGHT

A Cathedral: A Powerful Metaphor

"A cathedral is never finished, nor will it ever be. Just as human perfection is something we all strive for and can never be obtained, a cathedral will forever be changing, growing, crumbling. An ongoing legacy of our feeble efforts to touch God, a cathedral is neither a stone nor a statue or even a place of prayer. It is a continuum of creation; a beautiful work that I pray to God will never end."

Cathedral dedication by Prior Philip
from the book and movie
The Pillars of the Earth

BY DEFINITION, A CATHEDRAL IS a Christian church that contains the seat of a bishop. Cathedrals are indeed impressive structures, with the term "cathedral" often applied to any large and impressive church, regardless of whether it functions as a cathedral, to figuratively imply that a church is of outstanding beauty. The role of a cathedral is chiefly to serve God in the community and the building itself, by its physical presence, symbolizes both the glory of God and the church. A cathedral is frequently the most impressive building, and one of the most ancient buildings, in its town.

Because most cathedrals took centuries to build and decorate, they also constitute a major artistic investment for the city in which they stand, often housing treasures such as stained glass, statues, historic tombs, furniture and fine art. "The cathedral is both an architectural marvel and a shrine to human experience, in both its lowliest and most exalted. Indeed, it seems that the greatness of the cathedral is that it is a vast metaphor for humanity; diverse but striving toward harmony, grand but imperfect, and always a work in progress." (Matteson, 2002, p. 294 "Constructing ethics and the ethics of construction" in *Cross Currents* v52).

Cathedrals required teamwork on a scale never seen before or perhaps since. In addition to the regular daily workers contributing to the completion of a cathedral, it was expected in modern days for everyone to contribute. Doctors, lawyers, women and children all assisted without pay. In fact, offerings were often collected to pay for the cathedral. And from the moment the first stone was laid, they sparked an intense rivalry between cities, often resulting in war. Building a cathedral took blood, sweat, tears, muscle and vision. A cathedral was a gift to the future requiring a commitment to something larger than oneself. Each cathedral tells a story; each is as unique as the artists who played the roles of architect, builder, craftsman, designer and engineer. Using the simplest of tools, workers were able to construct some of the most amazing structures ever built.

These giant walls of glass in a kaleidoscope of colors have dominated skylights for nearly 1000 years. Many cathedrals are actually taller than the ancient pyramids in Egypt, and are large enough to hold the Statue of Liberty. Constructed of over 100 million pounds of stone, they are seemingly weightless, yet, are as heavy as the Empire State Building. Fueled by faith and guided by daring engineering, cathedral builders created sacred spaces that still inspire people to this day. Cathedrals have been referred to as "Heaven on Earth" and the light from the stained glass described as a symbol of God. Interestingly, experts are currently exploring a potential hidden mathematical code taken from the Bible (e.g., the Temple of Solomon, the height of The City referenced in Revelations, the dimensions of Noah's Ark) and used from the very beginning as a blueprint to build these massive structures.

A Cathedral:
A Personal Expression of Purpose

A cathedral is a powerful metaphor, with its stained glass and polished stone each telling a story and often taken for granted for their beauty. Most of us have and can identify with our own personal Cathedral that provides the motivation to keep us going and working toward something bigger than ourselves. A Cathedral, as we define it, is something that adds purpose to our lives, something that gets us out of bed each morning. A Cathedral can be something or someone that drives our behavior—our source of energy, our personal expression of purpose. And, that Cathedral may or may not be able to be built in our 9 to 5 jobs.

Cathedrals come in many shapes and forms. God is the ultimate Cathedral. Our family and our children are primary. Secondary Cathedrals could be our job, a project, an organization, etc. In short, we all need a Cathedral, a purpose, something that keeps us going, something to believe in, something to build. While most of us who seek eventually find our "Cathedral," in many cases God presents Cathedrals in the form of a special-needs child or when one finds oneself as an adoptive parent. Just as God spoke to Moses in the Old Testament, most parents of special-needs children would most likely agree they too have experienced a "burning bush" moment. In the following pages, we will introduce a few of these folks and many others who are building-modern day Cathedrals.

Questions for Consideration

- How would you describe a Cathedral?
- Why is a Cathedral such a powerful metaphor?
- Are there other metaphors that describe the power of purpose?
- What are your personal Cathedrals?
- Are you actively pursuing these Cathedrals with passion and purpose?
- What steps do you need to take in building your Cathedrals?
- Do you see your purpose as a Cathedral?
- Can your fires become the foundation of you becoming a Cathedral Builder?
- Do you think your employees/team members see their job as a Cathedral?
- What specifically could be done to create a Cathedral Builder culture in your organization?
- What specific Cathedral building traits do you see among the leaders in your organization?

MODERN-DAY CATHEDRALS

CHAPTER NINE

10,000 Cranes, One Cathedral

IN JAPAN, THE CRANE IS a mystical creature that is said to live a thousand years and, as the ancient Japanese legend goes, anyone who folds a thousand origami paper cranes will be granted a wish.

Kay Coomes's mother was born in Yokohama, Japan. Her father met her while serving in the Navy. He had been assigned to a post-World War II reconstruction crew working in Japan in the early 1950s. Being a Navy brat, Kay and her six siblings moved frequently, never making long-term friendships, which might explain why they are so attached to one another to this day. Kay's father was never home for any length of time; her mother, who barely spoke English, became their foundation, their Cathedral. Her mother was diagnosed with kidney cancer in 1986 and died within four months.

On March 3, 2011, a tremendous earthquake registering 9.0 produced a deadly tsunami that hit the northern part of Japan, killing tens of thousands of people. Kay, remembering her mother and feeling a strong sense to do something, began looking for a Cathedral to build in honor of both her mother and the Japanese people. She thought of Suko and the story of the origami paper cranes. Suko, a Japanese child of 12, suffered from radiation poison from the atomic bombs dropped at the end of World War II. She believed the ancient legend that said if she folded 1,000 paper cranes, she would be granted a wish of a healthy life and be healed. Suko died before she could complete her 1,000th crane, but the children of Japan rallied for her after her death and finished her project. This story resonates throughout Japan, and the origami paper crane now carries added significant meaning.

Kay found her Cathedral, a way of honoring her mother, by finding 10,000 people willing to make one origami paper crane and attach $1. She raised $10,000 for the American Red Cross and its international relief effort, and collected almost 30,000 inspirational origami cranes constructed for the Japanese people. There is indeed healing power in art, and Kay quickly teamed up with other organizations, with the result of their artwork eventually being displayed in Japan as an act of solidarity. Most importantly, Kay's Cathedral honored her mother while sending a strong message of love and hope to the Japanese people.

Questions for Consideration

- Is there a project, a Cathedral, that you have been thinking about building but for whatever reasons have yet to start? If so, why not?

- Is there a Cathedral that you should build in honor of a parent or someone of importance to you?

- What would cause you to start building that Cathedral today?

- Is there someone in your life that could use your help, your encouragement, and your support in building their Cathedral?

CHAPTER TEN

The Angel, the Cathedral Builder, and the Hero

THOSE WITH SPECIAL NEEDS are indeed "Angels from Heaven." They are full of love, express their feelings freely and are the epitome of sincerity. A friend of mine recalls an encounter she had with a young man with Down syndrome. This gentleman walked up to my friend and said, "You smell so pretty, like a flower." That Angel made my friend's day! Why are we so apprehensive to express our true feelings without the fear of being perceived as flirtatious or insincere? Why is it so difficult to accept praise without assuming that person wants something? But those with special needs never have to fear being accused of anything but love and sincerity. In fact, those with special needs don't worry about much of anything and are happy most of the time. God has sent these beautiful people to touch and inspire us, to give us an opportunity to demonstrate how we treat others.

I first learned of Roy Taylor when my son entered the eighth grade. Roy was a classmate and has Down syndrome. My son spoke frequently of Roy, about how "cool" he was, and how everyone protected him when other students occasionally made fun of him. My son was playing with Roy one day when a teacher thought my son was making fun of him. It wasn't the reprimand that bothered my son as much as the thought that anyone would ever think he would make fun of his friend Roy.

Thanks to Roy's perseverance, his dedicated teachers, and his loving friends and family, he received his high school diploma with my son and 250 classmates. Just a few weeks before graduation, my son told me, "Dad, when Roy walks up to receive his diploma, the entire graduating class is going to stand up and give him a standing ovation." That was the first of many times I would shed a tear thanks to Roy. The late Jim Valvano challenged us to do three things every day: Think, Laugh and Cry. He said if we could do these three things every day, that would be "a heck of a day" and Roy has been responsible for making a heck of a day for thousands of people.

The Angel

Right before Roy's name was called to receive his diploma, I made eye contact with my son. In anticipation of the standing ovation, I saw my son wipe the tears from his eyes. As the loudspeaker announced "Roy Taylor," not only did the entire graduating class jump to their feet, over 5000 family, friends and supporters rose to celebrate the accomplishment of one of God's Angels. There wasn't a dry eye in the crowd.

There was indeed a Cathedral Builder in Roy's life. His grandparents raised him after his father died in a drowning accident and his mother realized she was not equipped to raise an Angel. Raising Roy required a purpose, a vision and a tenacity nothing short of a Cathedral Builder. From the beginning, Roy's grandmother, Pat Taylor, would persevere even when others said Roy would never be able to function in society.

When the medical professionals would try to keep everyone's expectations reasonably low, Pat never lost faith. On numerous occasions, when doctors told her that it was "time to face facts, Roy will never walk or talk."

Pat boldly exclaimed, "Don't you ever tell me or another parent what their child can't or won't do! Roy will walk and he will talk!" Even after a very rough beginning, which included undergoing open-heart surgery when he was only six months old, Roy has exceeded everyone's expectations.

Roy had many friends throughout his school days, but none stood out like the hero he met in first grade. Savanah Satterly was a classmate of Roy's, and they immediately formed a bond. Teachers and classmates remember how, on many occasions, Savanah ended up in the principal's office for roughing up someone who had made fun of Roy. "Roy has made me a better person," says Savanah. "I am amazed how God can work so strongly through one person as he does through Roy. While I get the credit for helping Roy, he has helped, encouraged and supported me more than he or anyone else will ever know. He is my Angel."

Questions for Consideration

- What are the risks to expressing our true feelings?

- If I express my true feelings, what is the worst thing that can happen? What is the best thing that can happen?

- Why is it so difficult to accept compassion from others?

- What can we learn from those with special needs?

- What can we learn from those who care for those with special needs?

- What can we learn from Savanah?

- What characteristics does Savanah possess that can be useful for leaders?

- Why do some leaders consider "caring" as a "weakness" in leadership?

- Do you stand up for those who may need our assistance?

- Do you see the Cathedral potential in those with special needs? Why or why not?

- Are we using our leadership, popularity, blessings, and influence to set the example for how we treat others?

- Are we willing to risk our popularity in doing the right thing and making a stand?

CHAPTER ELEVEN

I Am the Child

Author Unknown

I AM THE CHILD who may not be able to do all the things you do. I am, however, very observant and can see whether you are happy or sad or fearful, patient or impatient, full of love and desire, or simply interacting with me out of duty. I marvel at your frustration, knowing mine to be far greater, for I cannot always express my needs or myself as easily as you do.

I can't always give you answers to your everyday questions or rewards as defined by the world's standards. What I do give you is much more valuable *And while you're at it*—I give you opportunities. You receive opportunities to discover the depth of your character, the depth of your love, your commitment, your patience, your abilities; the opportunity to explore your spirit more deeply than you imagined possible. I drive you further than you would ever go on your own, working harder, seeking answers to your many questions with no answers.

I am the child who may not be able to walk or talk with great ease. My gift to you is to make you more aware of your great fortune, your health, your ability to communicate, your ability to do for yourself. And while I may not learn as easily as you, what I do know is infinite joy in simple things. I am not as burdened as you are with the struggles and conflicts of a more complicated life. My gift to you is to grant you the freedom to enjoy things as a child, to teach you how much your arms around me mean, to give you love, to give you the gift of simplicity.

I am your teacher and if you allow me, I will teach you what is really important in life. I will give you and teach you unconditional love. I gift you with my innocent trust, my dependency upon you. I teach you about forgetting your own needs and desires and dreams. I will teach you about giving. Most of all, I will teach you hope and faith. I am The Child.

CHAPTER TWELVE

May He Touch Hearts

"THE GOOD NEWS IS YOU'RE PREGNANT, the bad news is I'm retiring," said the doctor to his 40-year-old patient with whom he had not only established trust; he had built a lasting friendship. While the earlier news that her trusted doctor would be retiring was disappointing, the news to come would be devastating. "Nancy, the test results strongly suggest that your baby has Down syndrome." Nancy Combow hoped the next step would be a referral to a specialist who would provide more information about Down syndrome and a heart-to-heart conversation about what one could expect and how best to build a Cathedral.

The beautifully decorated offices with modern paintings, expensive furniture and complimentary valet parking could not hide the insensitivity and barbaric counseling that would follow. The doctor began with a stoic definition of Down syndrome, a congenital disorder caused by the presence of an extra 21st chromosome, in which the affected person has mild to moderate mental retardation. He ended with a story about Forrest Gump, using words, anecdotes, negative images and scare tactics designed to tear down the Cathedral, a Cathedral whose foundation is barely 16 weeks old. But soon more destructive tools, modern but no less destructive than the medieval tools used by Vikings to destroy cathedrals hundreds of years ago, were introduced. Tools such as Extraction, Suction, D&C, and D&E that would terminate the pregnancy and in a manner that would satisfy the insurance companies.

Alarmingly, many reports suggest over 90% of prenatal diagnoses of Down syndrome are terminated. Because of the advances in the treatment and therapy of those with Down syndrome, it's never been a better time to be born with Down syndrome, but sadly, thanks to new tests that can diagnose Down syndrome as early as ten weeks, one has the least chance of actually being born. We don't always choose the Cathedrals that must be built, but we are responsible to make sure these magnificent structures touch the heavens.

Distraught, but determined to find someone who would deliver her Cathedral, she returned to her original doctor for a more appropriate referral. Her trusted doctor would not disappoint this time. The new referral's words were encouraging and his personal touch comforting. But it was his prayer as he laid his hands on her stomach that changed lives that day and set into motion the changing of many lives in the future. "May he touch hearts" was the simple, yet powerful prayer that was heard and granted by an amazing and awesome God!

Cameron is now six years old and touches hearts every day. His mother, Nancy, is indeed building a Cathedral to The Almighty.

Questions for Consideration

- Like Nancy, do we see our children or loved ones as Cathedrals?
- Are we building Cathedrals that touch hearts?

CHAPTER THIRTEEN

The following was originally delivered as a plenary address by Dennis McGuire, PhD at a conference in Chicago in July of 2005, co-sponsored by the National Down Syndrome Society and the National Association for Down Syndrome. Dr. McGuire is with the Adult Down Syndrome Center of Lutheran General Hospital, Park Ridge, Illinois. Used with permission.

What If People with Down Syndrome Ruled the World

- Affection, hugging and caring for others would make a big comeback.

- All people would be encouraged to develop and use their gifts for helping others.

- All people would be refreshingly honest and genuine.

- A stuffy high society would not do well in the world of Down syndrome.

- Big "dress-up" dances would flourish.

- Order and structure would rule.

- Schedules and calendars would be followed.

- Trains and planes would run on time.

- Lunch would be at noon. Dinner at 6 PM.

- Work time would be work time.

- Vacation would be vacation.

- People would be expected to keep their promises.

- Places would be neat, clean, and organized (not just bedrooms, but cities, countries, the whole world).

- There would be more tolerance for repeating the same question and arranging things until they are "just so."

- The words "hurry" and "fast" would not be uttered in a polite society. "Plenty of time" would take their place.

- Stopping to smell the roses would not be just a cliché.

- Work would be revered, no matter what kind, from doing dishes to rocket science.

- Weather would be the only essential news item and the news would be more local ("A new McDonald's just opened up," or "A dance tonight," etc.).

- Richard Simmons and John Travolta would be national heroes.

- Elvis, the Beatles, and the Beach Boys would still be number one on the hit parade.

- Musicals would be very, very, very big (such as *Grease*, and *The Sound of Music*).

- *I Love Lucy*, *Happy Days*, *The Three Stooges*, etc. would be very BIG.

- *Life Goes On* would also be very big and replayed regularly.

- Movie theaters would allow people to talk out loud and tell what happens next.

- People would not hurt the feelings of others, and they would also not lie or keep secrets.

CHAPTER FOURTEEN

Cathedrals, Cathedrals, Read All About It!

I OPEN THE NEWSPAPER to page 14 and the "Food Review" is titled, "Labor of Love." The writer describes how he grew up in the restaurant business, his parents owning several restaurants in South Carolina and Florida. He opines that it's not just the food one serves that matters, but also how one serves others. He provides a through overview of a restaurant owner who hails from Philadelphia and his head chef, whose famous Philly cheesesteak instantly makes your mouth water. It makes you want to check your calendar for the quickest opportunity to try this new restaurant. Is this a review from the Sunday *New York Times*? And who is the writer?

The paper isn't the *New York Times*. It is *The Contributor*, based in Nashville, Tennessee and the writer is Michael, formerly homeless and now selling *The Contributor* on the streets of Nashville. *The Contributor* is a street newspaper focusing on the issues surrounding homelessness and is sold by the homeless and formerly homeless individuals. *The Contributor* is a monthly publication and is the highest circulating street newspaper of its kind in North America.

The publication starts new vendors out with an ID badge and a starting equity of 15 free papers. They sell the papers on public sidewalks for $1 each, plus unsolicited tips. After that point, if they want to keep selling, they purchase papers for 25 cents each and resell for $1, keeping all the profit. *The Contributor* provides other opportunities to earn free papers for meeting sales goals, exceptional sales techniques, submission and publication in *The Contributor*, referring other vendors, and attending vendor meetings.

Andrew, the editor of *The Contributor*, is also a divinity student. He describes his personal mission as, "To make visible what's invisible. To make audible what's inaudible. To help reverse the silence when it comes to poverty and homelessness." He points to the front page of *The Contributor* where the official mission appears below the title: "Diverse perspectives on homelessness, genuine opportunities for advancement."

Andrew adds a third mission for *The Contributor*: "To create community between vendors and customers." He cites numerous examples of how people who normally turn a blind eye to the homeless have now connected to a vendor they see on a regular basis and with whom they have developed a friendship: "When they don't see Joe for a few days, I get a call asking about how he's doing, where he's been." Mission accomplished.

According to Andrew, people who are homeless live on what others have called "the margins of society," where most of us never go or have to see. When I stop at the bottom of my exit ramp, I can only ignore that gentleman so many times before the tug at my heart forces me to act, to go to "the margins" of society. I'm forced to get out of my car and walk to a wooded area just beyond the interstate and witness firsthand the cardboard home of that man I see every afternoon. I have to find out what his name is and where he's from and what, if anything, I can do for him.

Andrew, being a man of faith, discloses that at one time he thought it was his responsibility to bring Jesus to "the margins," to that cardboard house I had just visited days ago. He eventually realized that was impossible. He explained, "Jesus is already at the margins," referencing Matthew 25:35-40:

"For I was hungry and you gave me something to eat, I was thirsty and you gave me something to drink, I was a stranger and you invited me in, I needed clothes and you clothed me, I was sick and you looked after me, I was in prison and you came to visit me.' Then the righteous will answer him, 'Lord, when did we see you hungry and feed you, or thirsty and give you something to drink? When did we see you a stranger and invite you in, or needing clothes and clothe you? When did we see you sick or in prison and go to visit you?' The King will reply, 'Truly I tell you, whatever you did for one of the least of these brothers and sisters of mine, you did for me.'"

The Contributor clearly understands that Cathedrals come in many shapes and forms, and those who build them are equally diverse. While most are equipped and motivated to identify and pursue a Cathedral, others struggle to find purpose in life. Just as it is exciting to witness those who are pursuing their purpose, it may be more intense to see the pain at the other end of the spectrum, those who are searching but experiencing no real purpose in their life. While they seek a Cathedral that could perhaps use their skills, their talents, and their passion, many people never find that opportunity. *The Contributor* is providing purpose for over 400 homeless people in Nashville.

To learn more about *The Contributor* and the Cathedrals they are building, please visit them at www.thecontributor.org.

Beautifully Said...

The following is an email I received from Andrew after he and I talked about the Cathedral metaphor:

One thought that struck me over the last week or so when I was thinking about the "Cathedral" metaphor. I was thinking about the people who say they are laying brick, or simply working—those who don't think about the finished product. I've known a lot of people like that, especially poor and homeless people. For many of them, they're (sic) not being able to see the finished product sometimes has to do, not with their having an insufficient outlook on life, but with their being robbed of their ability to dream, to imagine. Poverty has a tendency to wear at people's minds. I say all this to say that I think the metaphor works, especially in that we give people the opportunity to see something bigger, to see beyond each day. But where I think we have to be careful is in subconsciously judging the person who can't see beyond the brick and mortar—because, in many cases, he's simply lost the resources, the means, by which he might see beyond it. And it isn't necessarily his fault. For some, living life one day at a time, in the present moment, is even a means of survival, until they can look any further. I hope The Contributor is a catalyst in helping people see beyond the minutia. But sometimes the minutia is all people have space in their imagination for—and for those people, we have to be present, open, and vulnerable until they're ready to look any further. Sometimes the miracles can even come in the minutia...in the bricks.

Questions for Consideration

- What can we learn from *The Contributor* and the people who work there?

- What can organizations learn from *The Contributor* and the people who work there?

- Have you ever gone to the "margins of society?" If so, how did it feel? How did it change your thinking? If not, what keeps us from going there?

- How, if at all, has your view of the homeless changed?

CHAPTER FIFTEEN

3.1 Miles to the Cathedral

MY ALARM GOES OFF AT 5:30 AM and my head literally feels like someone just took a sledgehammer to it. To make things worse, it is spitting snow and the temperature outside has to be below freezing, as evidenced by the heater that has not cut off the entire night. As I start to shower and get ready for another day, I have to admit I am not very motivated to go into work today. It's starting out to be a Bricklayer-type day. As I warm my car and edge out of the driveway, my defroster has not quiet eliminated the ice on the windshield. It's cold!

As I pull out of my neighborhood onto the busy street, I see a single light a few hundred yards in front of me. As I grow closer, I also see what looks like an orange flag waving and two small red lights. To my amazement, I see a motorized scooter with what looks like the happiest and most determined man alive. His name is David Gregory and he is the best example of the power of purpose and the innate desire to contribute I have ever seen. Three days a week David navigates more than three miles over every pothole, every inattentive motorist and every form of inclement weather to his job at the local WalMart, where he serves as a greeter. Dual emotions of both inspiration and shame overtake me. I am inspired for obvious reasons, and ashamed that I had been moaning and groaning since the alarm had gone off. I am ashamed that I have totally taken for granted the blessings of good health, and the honor and dignity of being able to work.

David is 59 years old and was born with cerebral palsy. His mother was in labor for 72 hours, and doctors told David's family that he would not live past 14 years old. David credits his mother for pushing him to be his very best and gives God all the honor and glory, as he was saved when he was only nine years old. While David received his high school diploma in 1971, he credits a camp in the woods of Kentucky for not only giving him purpose, but also for changing his life.

Camp KYSOC, located in Carrollton, Kentucky, was an accessible camp designed to meet the needs of individuals with disabilities. The camp opened over 50 years ago as an Easter Seals camp but has unfortunately closed due to lack of funding. Every summer from 1962 to 1996, David attended Camp KYSOC; in 1981 he became a camp counselor, a master Cathedral Builder. With a tear in his eye David tells me, "That camp changed my life. It gave me purpose. It was my Cathedral." For details on how you can support the reopening of Camp KYSOC, visit www.campkysoc. org.

David's message to others: "Don't give up, don't ever give up. My life's not been easy. I could never play football or basketball like the other kids, but I attended every game that I could and supported others." His message to young people: "You have to work. You can't start at the top. You have to work your way up. Don't make fun of anyone. You never know what could happen to you and you could be in a similar situation. I would like to thank Wal-Mart for the opportunity to build my Cathedral."

And whatever your thoughts are of WalMart, there is no better example of a corporation that provides thousands of people, both young and old, the opportunity to contribute and the opportunity to work. It gives them a source of dignity, for which we all strive.

Questions for Consideration

- What can we learn from David Gregory?
- What can we learn from WalMart?
- What examples do you have of "The Power of Purpose?"

CHAPTER SIXTEEN

Building a Cathedral to the Almighty

UNDERSTANDABLY, MOST PEOPLE would expect PGA Professional Kenny Perry's Cathedral to be a pristine 18-hole golf course with manicured fairways, undulating greens and breathtaking views. But Kenny Perry's Cathedral has walls of jasper, gates of pearl and city streets pure as gold and clear as glass. Kenny Perry's Cathedral is garnished with precious stones, foundations of alabaster and emeralds. And while Kenny Perry's Cathedral has a river as clear as crystal and a tree of life, there are no bunkers, no hazards and most importantly, no handicaps. You see, Kenny Perry's Cathedral is The Kingdom of Heaven. He donates a percentage of all his proceeds from winning golf tournaments to his church, Lipscomb University, and the support of many other Christian-based initiatives. And if you visit his Country Creek Golf Course in Franklin, Kentucky, you are likely to see him hosting the local Boy's and Girl's Club or a special -needs young adult on the driving range using golf clubs Kenny contributed.

With his victory at The Memorial Tournament in 2008, Kenny joined Tiger Woods as the only player to win the Jack Nicklaus tournament three times. He was the number one Ball Striker on the PGA Tour in 2005. In 2002, Kenny received the prestigious Charles Bartlett Award for his charitable contributions to the community.

He is also a member of the Western Kentucky University Hall of Fame.

In 2009, Kenny was awarded the Payne Stewart Award in recognition of his respect for the traditions of the game of golf and his commitment to charitable giving. Kenny was a member of the elite team of only 12 golfers who would represent the United States in the victorious 2008 Ryder Cup. Kenny Perry is indeed an amazing person and a golf legend, but most importantly, Kenny Perry is a Christian who gives back and helps others find their purpose and build their Cathedral.

Yet, almost 25 years ago, at the age of 26, his future was anything but certain. He had a young family to support and little money to make his third attempt to qualify for the PGA Tour. But just like the fire of 1666, someone and something significant emerged after setbacks. That significant person for Kenny Perry was a friend and elder at his church who advanced $5000 for one last shot at Q-school. The deal: If Kenny failed, he owed his friend nothing. But if he succeeded, he would agree to donate five percent of his tour earnings to Lipscomb University. That was almost 25 years ago and over $1.5 million in support for the Christian -based college!

Questions for Consideration

- What can we learn from Kenny Perry?
- Are you using your talents, gifts, and position to help others?
- Is there someone out there who you should be sponsoring and/or helping get started with his or her Cathedral Building?
- After your big wins in life, do you point to the Heavens and give thanks?

CHAPTER SEVENTEEN

Recognizing Cathedral Builders

MY DAD WAS A FACTORY WORKER and stood on a concrete floor for over 40 years. I often wonder if there was a Christopher Wren who asked my father, "What are you doing"? I could imagine the conversation. "Mr. Coker, you're not simply a tool and die maker: those tools and die that you're making for our company are used to assemble Harley-Davidson motorcycles, and based on your hard work, you're actually providing an opportunity for millions of people to enjoy leisure time on 'America's motorcycle.'"

I don't think there was a Christopher Wren at my dad's factory, and I don't remember my father talking much about the work he did. What I do remember, like it was yesterday, is what he did every day after he left that factory. After eight long hours of standing on that concrete floor, my father raised a tobacco crop for most of my childhood. The money that he made put my sister and me through college without him having to borrow one cent or us owing anything on our education. And while I knew my father was always proud of the quality of those tobacco crops, I always thought those long hours after standing on that factory floor was simply a way to make extra money for the family. Without realizing it, I had labeled my father as a Bricklayer.

Bill Coker stands in his tobacco patch out on Loving Chapel Rd. He raised eight acres of burley.

40 hours plus

JAMES L. HAMMER
Agricultural Consultant
Simpson County Bank

Bill Coker decided he could do more than 40 hours of labor in one week at Potter & Brumfield. Seeing an opportunity to lease some burley and dark tobacco acreage, Bill thought he had the time and workable knowledge needed to produce 8 acres of tobacco.

The crop was grown about 6 miles east of Franklin on the Loving Chapel Road on the Jr. Rippy Farm. He had an excellent yield for a dry summer. His burley variety selection was R7-11. To control weeds, he used Tillman (2 2/3 quarts per acre), for black shank and blue mold he used Ridomil (2 quarts per acre), for cut worms and wire worms he used diazinon (3 quarts per acre), and for flea beetles, Orthene at the rate of 1 pound per acre was used.

Observing the crop at cutting time, it was apparent the herbicides and insecticides had worked well for him. His fertilization followed recommendation as a result of soil testing. His dark tobacco was a Springfield, Tennessee experimental variety which has a small stalk and broad leaf. His 5.8 acres of dark sold out of the barn for $1.65 per pound.

At cutting and stripping time it was necessary for him to employ extra labor which was readily available this year. The burley crop of 3.2 acres weighed 2453 pounds per acre, a very good yield for 1983.

Bill and his wife, Barbara, live in the Macedonia Community after having moved here from Hartsville, Tennessee. Their daughter, Patty, works for the Defense Department in Washington and son, Greg, is a sophomore at W.K.U.

However, some 30 years later, my father removed a tattered newspaper clipping from his wallet and asked if I remembered the story in our local paper that featured his tobacco crop. As he unfolded that newspaper article and proudly handed it to his son, who had been preoccupied writing a book about others Building Cathedrals, I suddenly realized that the15 acres of tobacco my dad raised every year was more than just extra income for the family; it was my father's Cathedral. I am ashamed of overlooking this simple but very important distinction.

Not only do Cathedrals come in all shapes and sizes, they are built at all times of the day and very often outside of one's 9 to 5 job. My dad was a perfectionist, and his tobacco crop was not only the best in our county, it was always the best in the state. Some 30 years ago I sat impatiently in the cab of his pickup truck, watching him make numerous trips back to the barn to make sure every piece of tobacco was in its place. I remember becoming more and more frustrated and impatient. But now I realize that my dad wasn't simply raising 15 acres of tobacco. He was building a Cathedral that gave him purpose and one that still produces record yields in both our hearts.

Questions for Consideration

- Are there Cathedrals being built in our very back yard, right under our nose, that we have failed to recognize?

- Are we treating those who are "packing our parachute" like Bricklayers? How can you impact this "Bricklayer mentality?"

- Are we treating employees, friends and family members like Bricklayers, at the expense of helping them become Cathedral Builders?

- What could help them move from a Bricklayer mentality to a Cathedral Building mentality?

- Would the quality of their work, their Cathedral, improve if we simply acknowledged the importance of their work?

- How can we be better listeners when that Cathedral Builder is trying to tell us his or her passion and not let our non-verbal cues communicate that we're not that interested?

- The gentleman who wrote this article about my dad was my former high school agriculture teacher. The local bank hired Mr. Hammer after his retirement from the school system. The bank, to their credit, allowed Mr. Hammer to use his writing talent to recognize Cathedral Builders in the community. My father has banked at this institution for over 50 years and would never consider leaving. Customer loyalty is created when organizations and their employees recognize customer's Cathedrals and when employees perceive themselves as Cathedral Builders. Does your organization allow employees to use their passions to build customer loyalty and, more specifically, build Cathedrals?

- Is your organization a culture of Bricklayers or a culture of Cathedral Builders?

CHAPTER EIGHTEEN

"Any nation that does not honor its heroes will not endure."

—Abraham Lincoln

Someone Has to Tell the Story

Matthew Young, Director of Education,
National Infantry Foundation,
Columbus, Georgia

MY FATHER WAS IN THE VIETNAM WAR, both my grandfathers served in World War II, a great-grandfather in World War I, and many of my ancestors served in the American Civil War. I often wonder what would have happened if a bullet had strayed one foot to one side or the other, or perhaps if an artillery round fell just short of its target and one of my ancestors was killed or horribly wounded. The answer: I would not here today telling the story of millions who have served our country, protected our freedoms, and secured democracy.

I always dreamed of growing up and joining the military, continuing a family legacy. Because no one in my family had served as an officer, my father advised me when I was in high school that if I wanted to be in the military, I should go to college, join ROTC, graduate, and enter the officer ranks. He explained that it was better pay, better treatment, and simply offered more opportunities.

I followed his sage advice and entered ROTC in college, obtaining an ROTC scholarship that paid most of my tuition.

However, my junior year of college, I became very sick and had to drop out of school and ROTC. My first personal "fire" would be diabetes. The flames and smoke cleared and my rebuilding consisted of insulin, a new lifestyle, and going back to school. While I received my college degree, it would be without ROTC. Honestly, I didn't think the military would want a wounded soldier. However, I still had the burning desire to serve my country.

With a degree in history, I felt the call to serve my country by telling the story of all those who served before me. In 2008, I received my orders to serve as the Education Director of the National Infantry Foundation, which was in the process of completing the new National Infantry Museum at Ft. Benning in Columbus, Georgia. This amazing facility is dedicated to telling the stories of those who have served and are serving in the Infantry branch of the United States Army. The Infantry Museum is truly a Cathedral honoring the soldiers and their families who have sacrificed so much for their country. But a Cathedral is never finished; the journey of telling the story is never complete. And, if there's no one to tell the story of the Cathedral—why it exists, how it came to be, its purpose—we have a beautiful building, but an empty shell.

It's the stories of the men and women who served that make the museum, not the building itself, a true treasure. And while I couldn't serve in the military, it is an honor to tell the story to millions of people each year. One of the most rewarding feelings is to see the eyes of a child light up as he or she begins to comprehend the principles of loyalty, duty, respect, selfless service, integrity and personal courage.

As for my family, the legacy of service continues with my brother, who is scheduled to graduate from the United States Military Academy in the Class of 2013. I am so proud of him and of all the soldiers who volunteer everyday putting their lives at risk so that we remain a free nation. A Cathedral requires the skills of many artisans and one's assignment in building that Cathedral may not be the mission that we necessarily signed up for. In my case, God chose a different path. And while it wasn't the path I thought I would take, it was the one He meant for me to walk. My path is one of telling the story and one in which I encourage you to join me.

Go to www.nationalinfantrymuseum.com
for more information.

Questions for Consideration

- Why is this story so important to be told?
- What story should you be responsible for being preserved, for being told?
- How can your organization be more effective in telling its story for greater impact?
- How important is storytelling in organizations?

Seated: Greg Coker, author and Sherry Welch, editor. Standing: Bobby Clark, founder Clark Legacies, LLC, Will Peppers, graphic designer, and Dan Blake, president/COO, Integrated Media Corp.

CHAPTER NINETEEN

Helping Others Tell Their Story; Helping Others Build a Cathedral
Bobby Clark

FROM AN EARLY AGE, MY MOM taught me how important it is to help others. My father died in the crash of a small plane, which he was piloting, when I was eight years old. My mother had barely turned 17 years old when I was born; she dropped out of school before finishing the tenth grade. After my father's death—facing the daunting task of supporting three children under eight—she returned to school and became a secretary at an insurance company. My mother was an excellent provider and insisted that we go to college; there was no doubt that higher education was essential. The other most important thing my mother taught me by example—through her actions—was that helping others should always be an important part of our lives.

I wrote my first business plan while in graduate school after working in a campaign for governor. I learned Kentucky has more than 3,000 elected officials and didn't have a reliable directory that listed accurate information on all elected officials. Remember, this was at a time that the public had not heard of the Internet, let alone Google.

I have enjoyed my 25 plus years as an entrepreneur, publisher and small business advocate. My company has published a directory of the "who's who" of Kentucky government, business, and education officials. In 2005, we created and published the first *Kentucky Almanac* in more than 150 years: with written contributions from more than 180 Kentuckians including the late historian laureate Dr. Thomas D. Clark. The *Kentucky Almanac* became a bestseller, but what we are most proud of is the fact that the publication is a great resource for students and others who are also proud of our great Commonwealth.

A few years after the *Kentucky Almanac*, we decided to begin publishing books in a non-traditional manner. We had regularly received calls from those who wanted assistance publishing a novel or their family history, mainly because we are one of just a handful of Kentucky publishers. But we had always told them we only published our own books, and that we would not publish for individuals until we had the experience of marketing and distributing our own books in the retail bookseller world. We learned a lot and decided to expand by offering our book publishing services to others who had a story to tell.

At first, helping others share their legacies and their ideas through books was simply a marketing decision. The publishing industry was going through fundamental changes, with e-books, Internet sales, and major retailers undercutting the price on bestsellers. Small publishers often have production and printing expenses that mount up to more than these huge retailers are charging for the books they sell to customers.

In 2007, besides our usual publications, we published two books for other people: one for a good friend of mine and a poetry book for a friend of the co-owner of our publishing company. Soon, we designed and published two anniversary magazines, and we began creating publications that document history and legacies of businesses, institutions and professionals. We published books that told the story of O. Leonard Press, founder of Kentucky Educational Television (KET); Al Smith, former host of KET's *Comment on Kentucky*, and Fontaine Banks, who was chief of staff to two Kentucky governors and advisor to six.

Our authors have written books for children, advice for women entrepreneurs, and how-to books for improving business operations. The former Secretary of Kentucky's Education and Workforce Development Cabinet, Laura Emberton Owens, wrote a book sharing her experiences of laughter and tears, and offering a new perspective about life's inevitable moments through a parent's eyes. And now one of our latest publications is my friend Greg Coker's book, *Building Cathedrals: The Power of Purpose,* which you have in your hands.

The executive director of the University Press of Kentucky reports that they receive 2,400–2,500 manuscripts each year but only publish 60–80 books. We realized there was excellent material being written by authors who need and deserve an opportunity to "build their Cathedral" but who were running into various roadblocks in reaching their goals. Helping these people, who have both a burning desire and the passion to share their story, has become a personal mission for me. It is the Cathedral I must build.

This purpose derives from losing my dad so early and Alzheimer's taking my mom at 59 years old, before I could learn more stories about my family to share with my daughter.

If you would like assistance in telling your story or leaving a lasting legacy in the form of a book, simply call me at Clark Legacies, (800) 944-3995, or e-mail sbvclark@gmail.com.

CHAPTER TWENTY

While Some Cathedrals Must Be Built by Future Generations, We Have the Responsibility to Lay the Foundation

Greg Allen

IN THE LATE 1960s, EIGHT young African-American men took a stand that not only laid the foundation for a mighty Cathedral to be built, it was a stand that changed the face of athletics at Syracuse University, as well the face of college athletics across the country. Many know of the rich history of Syracuse University football in the 1960s and 1970s. It is a place where many football All-Americans played and went on to play in the NFL. Syracuse football greats include Jim Brown, recognized by some as the greatest running back ever; Ernie Davis, the first African-American to win the Heisman Trophy; Floyd Little, All-American, NFL Hall of Famer; Larry Csonka, All-American, NFL Hall of Famer; Jim Ringo, All-American, NFL Hall of Famer and many others.

Because of Syracuse's reputation as a football powerhouse, combined with a rich history of stellar academics, a high school athlete recruited by Syracuse would find it extremely difficult to find a reason not to sign on the dotted line immediately. So was the case in the 1967–1968, school year when Syracuse recruited nine African-American student athletes who were indeed modern-day "Cathedral Builders." Of the nine, one was dismissed from the team for medical reasons and did not begin spring practice in 1970. Eight of us walked off the field in the spring of 1970 to protest discrimination, thus the title "Syracuse Eight." There were two other African-Americans on the team who chose not to participate in the boycott.

As with most highly recruited high school athletes, the Syracuse Eight had numerous colleges from which to choose, with individual stories that varied based on demographics. We were from different states; different communities, different family structures, different sizes, shapes, and positions but we had a common set of values that necessitated each of us taking a stand. Each of us wanted an opportunity to grab the brass ring, to elevate ourselves, our families and our futures. We were seeking the American dream through athleticism and intellect. We wanted to graduate with a diploma from one of the most prestigious schools in the country and go on to play in the NFL. Most of us would be the first-generation college graduates in our immediate families. And with many other African-American student athletes before us having found success at Syracuse, it seemed like not only a great opportunity, but also a dream within reach.

It's important to understand and reflect on what was going on culturally and politically during this time, in both our country and our world. College students across the country were protesting the Vietnam War. Students across the nation were becoming more politically aware of what was going on and wanted a voice in the direction in which the country was going. The Civil Rights era of the 1960s was fresh in everyone's mind. A new era and a new political discourse was unfolding in America. And for young African-American athletes, people like Muhammad Ali, who took a stand for what he believed in, were exemplary. We had the image of Tommy Smith and John Carlos on the Olympic medal stand making a political statement, knowing it was going to cost them dearly. We still had the example of Martin Luther King, Jr. as an ever-shining example of the possibilities of how to peacefully achieve lasting change. There was a renewed sense of pride in what is more commonly referred to as the black community. In fact, my story is not one of individuals as much as it is a story of where we were as a society, where we were as a culture, where we were as a nation, and why change was so inevitable.

I chose to attend Syracuse for the very same reasons as enumerated above. I had quite a few offers from Division I schools from which to choose. I think it's important to also point out that, in addition to the reasons listed above, I chose Syracuse for another reason. On my recruiting weekend I met another African-American recruit, John Lobon, from Hartford, Connecticut. We became instant friends and decided if one of us signed on, we both would sign on. John is my best friend to this day some forty-four years later. Iron indeed sharpens iron.

When I arrived in Syracuse in the late summer of 1968, I was met at the airport by one of my coaches. We picked up my belongings and headed to campus. Along the drive, which probably took less than fifteen minutes, the coach told me how glad they were that I had chosen Syracuse and that they wanted me to receive a great education, graduate, and make a real contribution to the football team. He told me that several athletes had gone on to the pros from Syracuse and he thought that might be a possibility for me. He told me to enjoy my college life but he also wanted to let me know that I wasn't to date any "white female coeds" while I was there. Needless to say, I was a little taken aback by the comment, but because that wasn't the reason I came to Syracuse, I didn't dwell on it.

We started pre-season practice before the varsity team arrived and everything was going well. As I met other African-American football players, I soon realized they too had had the conversation with the coach regarding dating white female coeds. We all noticed and were surprised by many of the procedures that seemed to only apply to black ballplayers. When it came time for me to register for fall classes, I registered with biology as my major. I did so because I was in an advanced biology curriculum in high school and had interned at the local hospital in my hometown because of my interest in biology. I was assigned to a biology course that had several labs a week. When I told my coaches that I needed to be excused from practice at a certain time to complete my lab work, they refused and suggested I re-register and drop my biology major. I was met by a student adviser who registered me as "general education." I eventually registered as a communications major in what is now the renowned Newhouse School of Communication. There were other black ballplayers who were redirected from their initial majors as well. A black engineering major was quickly told he, too, must change his major. Incidentally, we knew of several white ballplayers who were excused because of similar lab work and academic obligations.

There was also an issue regarding playing time and positions with several black players prevented from trying out. Normally, one might think that may have been the quarterback position, but Syracuse had a history of Black quarterbacks. Case in point: I had a good spring game and ended up running from the tailback position. When spring practice ended, I was solidly the second-team wingback, alternating with the first team. I went home for the summer, worked out intensely, and returned in excellent shape. In fact, while at Syracuse I was always the fastest on the team. When I arrived back at school, I found that the first-team wingback had quit school because of personal issues at home. Needless to say, I was sure I would move up to first-team wingback. That was not the case.

The fourth-team tailback was moved to first-team wingback. Naturally, I was shocked. Sure, he was taller and a little heavier than I but so was the former wingback when we were competing in the Spring. I approached my position coach and asked why I wasn't moving up to first-team in light of earning second-team status just two and half months ago without any scrimmages or practices in the interim. His response was the newly named starter, who was a former tailback, had been in summer school and was working out all summer and learning the plays. I said,

"Coach, it seems like I'm being penalized for not going to summer school." He said, "You're not starting, but you'll get a chance to play." Needless to say, I was very disappointed but told myself to suck it up and prove them wrong.

I practiced everyday like it was game day, and when they called first-team they called me to come along as well. Just two weeks from opening day against Iowa State, the new starting wingback found himself in trouble and was dismissed from school. Naturally, I assumed I was going to be the starter. Much to my chagrin, they moved the reserve fullback to first team wingback. I couldn't believe it—and to add insult to my injury, they asked me to help him learn the wingback assignments so he would be ready for the game. I went up to my position coach after practice and said, "Coach what's going on? How come you refuse to let me start?" He told me they wanted to go with experience. I said, "I know he's a junior, but you were going to let the new wingback start, and he was a sophomore just like me, and the starting tailback is a sophomore, so I don't understand this thing about experience." He replied, "Look, that's the way it is, and if you don't like it you don't have to play at all."

Not surprisingly, all the ballplayers that were moved ahead of me were white. For me, there was only one reason why I wasn't allowed to start and that was because I was black. This is not to say that there weren't white ballplayers that were treated unfairly at times as well. One of the issues we all had in common was poor medical treatment. Our team doctor was not an orthopedic. He was a general practitioner. Additionally, there are numerous stories of racial epithets, instances of racial overtones and retaliation for any involvement that appeared to be in the spirit of racial harmony.

I was approached by a group of African-American students to join them in meeting with university administrators to discuss securing an African-American studies program similar to the one recently put together at Cornell University, just down the road from Syracuse. It was a good meeting with no adversarial issues.

However, two days later I received a note from the head coach that he wanted to see me. I thought nothing in particular about him wanting to see me. Perhaps there was a pro scout in town or he just wanted to talk about spring practice. I sat down in his office and he asked me, "What's this black %&#@ you're involved in?" I responded, "Coach if you're talking about the meeting with administration it's about a Black Studies program that we would like to see implemented at Syracuse, just like at Cornell." He then instructed me I needed to make a decision: either I was going to be black or be a football player.

With all of us having similar stories and witnessing blatant racial injustice, we attempted to resolve these issues in a civil manner. Initially, we asked for the hiring of a black coach so we would have an advocate and someone with whom we could discuss our grievances. We proposed this to our head coach, and he agreed to consider and get back with us. We followed up with him several times, with him refusing each time. We felt we needed to make a statement that would communicate the seriousness of the situation. Ultimately, we decided to boycott. We felt that it was our moral obligation to take a stand, bringing this into the open with the hope the inequalities would stop. We knew inaction would only ensure others would suffer the same injustice. We knew we were risking any hopes of realizing our childhood dreams of playing in the NFL but ultimately had to ask this question: What is more important: our personal desires or our obligation to take a stand for justice and truth?

We knew in our hearts and believed that, "To whom much is given, much is required." We knew that to turn away and not help to effectuate change was a dereliction of our moral responsibilities not only to black ballplayers but to all athletes and to all mankind. It is important to note that of the eight, five of us were starters. I was the first-team tailback on the depth chart. I knew what I was giving up, as did the rest. There are moments in everyone's life when we are faced with decisions about doing what's right for one's self or doing what's right for the greater good even if there's a significant cost in helping others. Very often, and with us, "You don't pick history; history picks you."

The decision to boycott was no doubt painful. But I was raised by two parents who taught me above all else, it's what you do for others that's the true test of one's character. I believe God has ordained people for certain tasks and that each of us has a purpose. I believe the eight of us who boycotted, as well as our brother who was dismissed for medical reasons, were there by providential circumstances. We had to tear down the wall of injustice and erect a Cathedral of racial equality.

As we sat around the room making our decision to boycott, we all thought of the impact it would have on our families. We knew their hopes and dreams for us would be affected. They wanted their sons to obtain a college education, to fulfill their personal dreams, and to grasp those stars they so greatly deserved. Knowing this, we all pledged that no matter what happened, we would all graduate. We presented the coaches a list of demands that needed to be met in order for us to return. This was important because we were promised a black assistant coach several times in the past, with no follow-through. But the boycott wasn't just about us. We knew we had an opportunity to make things better for all of our teammates. Our demands were the following:

- The hiring of a black assistant coach.
- Better academic advisement and academic assistance.
- Players had the freedom to try out for any position on the team.
- Better medical treatment through the use of specialists.

It had nothing to do with playing time. It was about fair and equitable treatment. We felt that the hiring of a black assistant coach was a crucial first step and would begin to narrow the racial divide. For this reason, we did not specifically address any of the racial implications in our demands. The Chancellor of the university formed a commission to investigate our allegations. After months of interviews and testimonies, the commission, made up of faculty, administrators, and local government officials produced a 38-page report calling the ordeal "an act of institutional racism unworthy of a great university." While we were vindicated, our story didn't end there. Because of our stand against the establishment, we were all blackballed from the NFL, and while we all graduated, there were casualties.

One of our brothers went into a state of deep depression and once he left school, no one, including his family, ever heard from him again. The rest of us went on and received advanced degrees, becoming very successful in our chosen fields. And like in any story, there are more details and events that occurred. We'll cover these in a book soon to be completed. When I reflect back on these events and times, I am amazed at how a band of brothers, nineteen and twenty-year-olds, understood our unique calling in history, and, most importantly, took action. We not only changed the face of athletics at Syracuse University, we also changed the face of athletics nationally.

While we laid the foundation for a beautiful Cathedral, a Cathedral of racial harmony and justice, it is far from being built. Perhaps our children and grandchildren will finish this Cathedral. There are many signs of hope. Our children and grandchildren do not seem to view differences as the dividers our generation erected. But while we're not the ones who will complete the Cathedral, we have the opportunity, we have the *responsibility* to lay the foundation. I am reminded of King David in the Bible, who would not be the one to build the temple, but his son Solomon did. Racial harmony is a temple worth building, worth taking a stand, worth making a difference. Racial equality is coming. We just have to be patient and build it one brick at a time. Please join me in building this wonderful Cathedral.

The following article appeared in *University Place,*
a Syracuse University magazine

Return of the "Syracuse Eight" by *David Marc*

In 1970, at the heart of an era marked by the greatest political turmoil ever to hit American campuses, nine African American members of the Syracuse University football team, all scholarship players, petitioned the athletic program with a series of grievances. They wanted positive changes: medical care focused on student health rather than game-day readiness; academic support that recognized their status as students as well as athletes; unbiased assignment of starting positions; and racial integration of the coaching staff. Ignored, they chose to sit out the season, effectively ending their collegiate sports careers and their chances to play professionally.

On October 20, the "Syracuse Eight" (a miscount that stuck in the media) returned to campus to receive the Chancellor's Medal, one of the University's highest honors. Before a packed house at the Whitman School's Lender Auditorium, Chancellor Nancy Cantor welcomed the honorees to what she described as a "healing" experience, apologizing to them and praising them for standing up for their beliefs and enduring the hardships that followed. She noted that in the years following their refusal to play, the University addressed every point in their petition, making Syracuse University a national model for athletic program reform. "Your courageous effort, your courageous stand, supported by the dedication of the faculty and staff who ardently backed you—some of whom are here today—gave the process of change its essential push," she said. "The initial result was a statement for history by the University's investigative committee that cited 'institutional racism unworthy of a great university.'"

Hosted by Atlanta television journalist Angela Y. Robinson, '78, the event drew prominent alumni to campus, including football greats Jim Brown, '57, and Art Monk, '80. In 1970, Brown came to Syracuse to support the players and spoke on their behalf on national television. Visibly stirred by his reunion with them, an impassioned Number 44 challenged contemporary athletes to follow their example. "Who in sports today has shown the backbone and concern for the community these guys displayed 36 years ago, as college kids?" Brown asked.

As the story of the Syracuse Eight unfolded, interest grew from local coverage to an Associated Press story, distributed nationwide, headlined "School Honors Players' Anti-Racism Stand." Articles also appeared in The Sunday *New York Times* and *Jet*, a popular African-American weekly. Rami Khouri 70, G'98, editor at large for *The Daily Star* in Beirut, was on campus to participate in the international peace summit earlier that week. He stayed for the Syracuse Eight ceremony and found lessons in the reconciliation for his war-plagued region. "The episode reveals one of the best aspects of American culture: the determination to acknowledge the sins, crimes, or just transgressions of the past, as a means to fostering peace and stability in society," he wrote in *Middle East Online.*

John Lobon, '73, a defensive lineman for the 1970 Orange, is today a senior executive with the Connecticut Development Authority and a member of the state's Commission on Human Rights and Opportunities. "I forgave Syracuse University long ago...," he said. "But now I can make it part of my soul."

Greg Allen, a 1973 graduate of Syracuse University, earned a varsity letter in football (1969 and 1972) and in track in 1968. A member of the Athletic Governing Board and an honorary member of Sigma Alpha Mu, Greg Allen earned a degree from the Newhouse School of Public Communication and a certificate from Syracuse University Graduate School of Sales and Marketing Management. After a successful thirty-three-year career at Liberty Mutual, Greg Allen retired in 2009. A 2006 recipient of the Chancellor's Medal for Courage and the 2009 recipient of Syracuse University's Letterman of Distinction Award, he still holds the individual punt return record for a single game set in 1969, against Penn State. Having served and chairing numerous boards and committees, Greg Allen has been a general manager of a semi-pro football team and the head coach of championship youth football, basketball and baseball teams. Additionally, he has volunteered countless hours to civic organizations, prison ministries, and soup kitchens, and is a deacon at the Second Baptist Church of Elgin, Illinois. Greg has been married to his wife Sirena for forty years and they have three children, Tamika, Damian and Monika. Greg and his wife live in Chicago.

Questions for Consideration

- Specifically, what can we learn from Greg Allen and the "Syracuse Eight"?
- How would you have reacted if you were in Greg Allen's and his teammates' shoes?
- How would you have reacted if you were one of the white ball players? Would you have taken a stand with the "Syracuse Eight"? Would you have had the courage?
- What keeps us from taking a stand?
- What did Greg Allen and the "Syracuse Eight" give up by taking a stand for justice?
- What did they gain?
- How have things changed since the 1970s regarding racial harmony?
- Do you think your generation will complete his Cathedral (Racial Harmony), or will it be left up to our children/grandchildren's generation? Explain.

- What injustice have you suffered and how did you react? Have you forgiven, as John Lobon has?

- What opportunities exist today for you, and perhaps your family, to lead reform efforts?

Send examples of the Cathedrals you're building to mycathedral@thecathedralinstitute.com.

THE BRICKLAYERS

CHAPTER TWENTY-ONE

The First Bricklayer

WHEN I THINK OF the first bricklayer, I think there are generally three particular types. One type is the occasional bricklayer, who for the most part is able to pull herself/himself back to seeing the cathedral or at least seeing the wall. The next type is what I call the "salt of the earth" bricklayer. He or she has a good attitude, will give you an honest day's work for an honest day's pay, but view the job as simply a job. The third type of bricklayer is generally disengaged, simply "punching the clock" and stuck in bricklayer status.

Like many employees today, the first bricklayer Christopher Wren encountered was clearly "disengaged." The 2011 Employee Engagement Report, conducted by the global consulting firm Blessing White, found:

- Fewer than 1 in 3 employees (31%) are engaged and nearly 1 in 5 (17%) are disengaged.

- More and more employees seem to be looking for opportunities outside their current employer.

- Employees view opportunities to apply their talents as top drivers of job satisfaction.

- Trust in executives (The Christopher Wren in an organization) can have more than twice the impact on engagement levels than trust in immediate managers. However, employees are more likely to trust their immediate managers than the executives in their organization; reinforcing the need for MBWA (management by walking around) demonstrated by Wren.

- Relationships trump skills, that is, employees' knowledge of their managers as "people", appears to impact engagement levels more than actions alone.

- Less than two-thirds (61%) of respondents say they plan to remain with their organization through the next 12 months.

- Employees tend to flee bad managers, although they will not necessarily stay around for a good one.

Blessing White identifies five levels of engagement that describe the first bricklayer. This level, appropriately named "The Disengaged," is described as not necessarily starting out as "bad apples" of even being "bad apples" now, but most likely feel disconnected from organizational priorities and often feel underutilized, not getting what they need out of work. They're likely to be skeptical and indulge in contagious negativity.

Full engagement, on the other hand, occurs at the alignment of maximum job satisfaction and maximum job contribution. Contrast these two variables with Bricklayer 1, 2, and the Cathedral Builder. Unfortunately one doesn't need a formal survey for proof of employee disengagement in today's workplace. Just simply walk the halls and catch a glimpse of employees' computer screens, as workers peruse a host of non-business websites and social media.

The Christopher Wrens of corporate America are not immune from disengagement. Blessing White suggests executives must monitor and manage their engagement, or risk the entire organization suffering, as they tend to be the gatekeepers of the company culture. Many executives report feeling trapped in leadership roles that no longer provide challenge, meaning, or purpose—but given their executive pay and the struggling economy, quickly realize they can't afford to leave at this point. Organizations may feel safe now, regarding top management retention, but may be in for a real shock when the economy recovers and many top performers leave for opportunities that provide more meaning and purpose, for significantly less money. According to the research, less than half of directors and vice presidents are actually engaged.

Questions for Consideration

- If you're honest with yourself, which Bricklayer are you most likely to align with?

- What are the reasons for someone viewing them selves as Bricklayers versus Cathedral Builders?

- What can we do to help others see themselves as a Cathedral?

- In your organization, family, friendship, etc., do you feel there are more Cathedral Builders or more Bricklayers? Why?

- How engaged are you? Your employees/team members? Your family members?

- What are the key reasons for employee disengagement?

- What are the key reasons for family disengagement?

- How do we get employees/family members engaged?

- How important is "culture" in your organization?
- Describe the Christopher Wrens in your organization.

The Dynamics Between
The Two Bricklayers

"Two are better than one, because they have a good reward for their labor. For if they fall, one will lift up his companion. But woe to him who is alone when he falls, for he has no one to help him up."

—Ecclesiastes 4:9-10

WE CANNOT UNDERESTIMATE the dynamics between two or more bricklayers and the influence they have on each other. In fact, negative workplace relationships may be a big part of why so many employees are not engaged with their jobs. The first bricklayer in the story is clearly "actively disengaged." Gallop describes these employees as not just simply unhappy at work; they may be busy acting out their unhappiness. Every day these workers have the potential to undermine what their engaged co-workers accomplish. The *Gallop Management Journal*'s Employee Engagement Index places the current percentage of truly "engaged" employees at only 29%. A slim majority, 54%, fall into the "not engaged" category, while 17% of employees are "actively disengaged."

The second bricklayer in our story could at least "see the wall." Gallop categorizes this bricklayer as "not engaged." These employees are essentially "checked out." They're sleepwalking through their workday, putting time—but not energy or passion—into their work.

Gallop also analyzed workplace friendships and found that engaged employees are more likely than others to say that their organization "encourages close friendships at work." They found a very close correlation between engaged employees and the relationship with their manager, suggesting that managers who want to boost workgroup engagement levels—and help the not-engaged employees become engaged—might benefit from developing trusting and supportive relationships with their employees. Personal relationships seem to be a key to employee engagement.

In contrast, actively disengaged employees seem especially disenchanted with their connection with their manager. Naturally, engaged employees are much more likely to consider their relationship with their manager to be crucial to their success.

Gallop found that of all U.S. workers 18 or older, about 22.5 million—or 17%—are actively disengaged estimating the lower productivity of actively disengaged, workers costs the U.S. economy about $300 billion a year. (Gallop Organization Research Q3 2004)

Questions for Consideration

- What are the dynamics between two or more Bricklayers?

- What role do you play in assisting that Bricklayer see the Cathedral?

- How important are friendships in the workplace?

- How does your friendship with your boss impact your performance? With your direct reports? With your team members?

- What are some simple steps/activities that could enhance workplace friendships (employee outings, cookouts, sports, etc.)?

CHAPTER TWENTY-TWO

The Right People On the Bus,
In the Right Seats
and the Wrong People Off the Bus

IN THE BOOK *GOOD TO GREAT*, Jim Collins suggests great leaders get the right people on the bus, the right people in the right seats, and the wrong people off the bus.

Questions for Consideration

- Should the first Bricklayer be on the bus? Is he simply disengaged or has his immediate manager failed to properly orient him to the organization's mission, vision, goals, and objectives? Perhaps his job may not require him to see the Cathedral.

- How, if possible and if necessary, can we assist this bricklayer in transitioning to at least seeing the wall and ultimately seeing the Cathedral?

- Are we satisfied with this bricklayer staying in this status? We may be if he is a temporary employee, contractor, etc.

> - Is this an isolated case with the first bricklayer or a trend of many others feeling like bricklayers?
> - If it isn't an isolated case, is there a root cause for a culture of Bricklayers?
> - Has this Bricklayer been beaten down into this status by a toxic manager?

Ultimately, we might have to get this bricklayer off the bus altogether. Collins suggests that when we don't, we're actually being unfair to that person. "Every minute you allow a person to continue holding a seat when you know that person will not make it in the end, you're stealing a portion of his/her life, time that he/she could spend finding a better place where he/she could flourish."

The second Bricklayer may deserve a seat on the bus, but is he in the right seat? Could another more appropriate seat provide more of an opportunity to see and build a Cathedral?

Maybe Your Bus Has Changed

THERE ARE MANY CATHEDRALS out there to be built. They may not be the glitzy, shiny and the tallest Cathedral you may have been accustomed to building before the economy went south, but your current job may nonetheless be a Cathedral worthy of your time, your commitment, your passion. In the worst economy since the Great Depression, many people are performing jobs they may have never imagined they would be doing, and for substantially less money. Many have convinced themselves they are simply laying bricks, making themselves and others miserable complaining and completely failing to see the potential Cathedral they could be building if they would just be open to changing their mindset. The bricks could be in your mind.

Questions for Consideration

- How can getting the wrong people off the bus improve the Cathedral?
- General thoughts about getting the wrong person off the bus.
- How do we find the right seat on the bus? How do we assist others in finding the right seat?
- Has your bus changed?
- Do you know others whose bus has changed? How have they handled this?

What About the Driver?

WHAT ABOUT THE DRIVER OF THE BUS? You could have the right people on the bus, in the right seats, but the wrong driver in the form of a toxic manager. Unfortunately, no one at corporate notices the driver—or worse—they turn their heads because this driver runs an extremely efficient operation. Everyone on the bus and everyone at the division level is afraid and intimidated to let anyone know about this toxic manager for fear of retaliation. Revenues are great, the operation appears to be running smoothly, but the driver has created a culture of fear and intimidation, and corporate simply turns a blind eye to it.

Unfortunately in most organizations, operational results win out over culture every time. Management triumphs leadership in most situations with most organizations "over managed" and "under led." Operations managers tend to be promoted over marketing, public affairs, or human resources, even though the latter disciplines may be more suited for leadership. An engineer who is a wonderful operator may not be the best president.

Trucking companies clearly understand the mission to deliver customer freight from point A to point B. However, they realize there's another important variable in the "Cycle of Service." The most important question is one that many companies fail to ask: How's my driving? As long as the bus leaves the station on time, arrives at its destination on time, returns, keeps expenses to a minimum and profits high, ignoring the behavior of the driver doesn't seem that big of a risk. But the toxic driver will eventually destroy company culture, profits, and employee morale.

"Keep away from people who try to belittle your ambitions. Small people always do that, but the really great make you feel that you too, can become great."

—Mark Twain

Emotional Intelligence

THE DRIVER MAY BE BRILLIANT, well educated, get results, and look great on paper, but may never be able to harness the power necessary to create the appropriate culture, develop and maintain organizational trust, and achieve true success. The reason may have to do with a concept called Emotional Intelligence (EI). And while it may be harder to identify and measure than IQ, its power cannot be denied.

Emotional Intelligence (EI)—how we handle ourselves and our relationships—coupled with IQ, determine life and career success. Most of us have witnessed someone with extremely high IQ but extremely low EI crash and burn. In fact, it is often said many executives are hired on their expertise and fired on their personality. Daniel Goleman's bestseller *Primal Leadership* makes the point that a leader's emotions are contagious, resonating energy and enthusiasm, all playing a crucial role in the success of an organization. The converse is true. If the driver of the bus spreads negativity, mistrust, fear, and intimidation, the organization will eventually crumble.

Travis Bradberry and Jean Greaves in The Emotional Intelligence Quick Book, connect EI with job title and their findings are both surprising and alarming. EI scores rise from front-line supervisors to middle management, but beyond middle management, there is a steep decline, in EI scores. For the titles of director and above, scores sharply decline with CEOs on average having the lowest EI scores. Like the "bus driver" in our previous example, too many leaders are promoted because of what they know, financial/operational results, or tenure, rather than skill in leading others. Bradberry and Greaves found that EI skills are more important to job performance than any other skill, with those high in EI scores outperforming their peers.

Questions for Consideration

- Does the culture of your company value results over culture? If so, how does this impact Cathedral Building?
- What safeguards are in place to keep the crazed driver from destroying morale, employee engagement, and in general making life miserable for everyone and impacting the building of the Cathedral?
- Can you and your organization afford not to ask the question, "How's my driving?"
- As a leader, are you committed to peak performance to ask the question, "How's my driving?"
- Do you have the self-confidence to ask the question, "How's my driving?"
- How would you rate your EI score?

- What happens to your organization's EI scores the higher you go up the corporate ladder?

- Where in your company are high EI scores most important?

- How is your company developing the EI of its employees?

Helping the First Two Bricklayers
See the Cathedral

A *PERSONNEL TODAY* SURVEY (July 2008) of 350 human resources professionals found that the greatest factor in workplace productivity is a positive environment in which employees feel appreciated. According to the survey, two thirds of the respondents said they felt significantly more productive when they received recognition for their work, while the remainder said they felt in general more productive.

Just simply feeling productive can actually be a motivator. When employees don't feel productive, frustration sets in, according to 84 % of the survey respondents. In fact, 20 % said they felt angry or depressed when they weren't able to work as hard as they could. In short, most employees desire and will see the "Cathedral" if we simply create an environment for them to do so.

CHAPTER TWENTY-THREE

Creating a Culture of Cathedral Builders

- View the new employee orientation process as one of the most important opportunities to communicate the organization's mission, vision, goals, objectives, priorities, and guiding principles, and have it delivered by senior management.

- Structure and schedule follow-up on the above, keeping the Cathedral in full view.

- Be sincerely interested in your employees as people as well as team members.

- Spend the first 10 minutes of everyday simply walking around and saying good morning (MBWA). Can't afford to spend this much time every morning? You can't afford not to!

- Appreciate what others bring to the table. You may be an engineer and a bottom-line, no-nonsense type of a guy, while your direct report is a right-brained public relations professional. Appreciate and value differences.

- Build, maintain, and understand the dynamics of your team. Teams go through predictable stages of growth. Recognize, manage, and own each team-building stage:

➢ Form: when a team is just learning to deal with one another.

➢ Storm: a time of stressful negotiation of the terms under which the team will work together.

➢ Norm: a time in which roles are accepted, team starts to develop, and information is freely shared.

➢ Perform: optimal levels are finally realized—in productivity, quality, decision-making, allocation of resources, and interpersonal interdependence.

➢ Transform: the transformation from a culture of bricklayers to a culture of Cathedral Builders.

- Establish, nurture, and maintain trust. If you've given someone feedback only to feel the person never heard and/or acted upon it, check the trust level between you and that person. Trust has to be present for feedback to be received and implemented.

- Give immediate feedback versus storing it up for a performance appraisal. People hate surprises, and storing up this feedback for months only creates animosity. If you have constructive feedback, give it and move on. Avoid "poop sandwiches" where you give a little positive, a little negative, and then end with a little more positive. If you do this on a regular basis, no one will ever hear the positive because he or she knows what will follow and is still thinking about what just happened while you're delivering the positive feedback at the end of this less-than-effective performance appraisal.

- Utilize the talent of your employees. The worst feeling in the world is wanting to get in the game and contribute but the coach is ignoring you. In fact, the worst thing you can do to someone is to ignore him or her. It may have worked on the playground when you were a child, but in the workplace the results are much more damaging.

- Treat your employees as colleagues, sparring on an equal basis. They know who's boss and if you treat them with respect, they'll not exploit the relationship. Remember the transition from high school to college, when certain professors started treating us like adults? This was liberating as well as motivating, and we didn't stop going to class and become disengaged. On the contrary, we started sitting up front, participating more—and our grades drastically improved!

- Be interested, understanding, and supportive of your employees' life outside the workplace. Ask them about their family! Know their children's names and what they're involved in. Encourage them in building their cathedral.

- Create the appropriate amount of tension. A popular metaphor is that of a rubber band, which represents the challenge we need and want in our jobs. Imagine pulling a rubber band between your two index fingers. If it's too loose, you're not challenged and will become bored. If the rubber band is stretched too tight, you're stressed and more likely to burn out. If there's an appropriate amount of tension, you're challenged and are more likely to achieve peak performance. Athletes call this the zone or flow. Create it with your team!

- Strive for respect, not fear. If your employees fear you, both you and the organization lose. "Group think" sets in, and your employees will never speak up for fear of retaliation. The concern for senior-level managers who have managers reporting to them should be to make sure their direct reports are not toxic, with direct reports afraid to "take on the king/queen" and risk not killing him/her. In this case, the Christopher Wren needs to monitor and seek feedback on his/her managers. He or she needs to leave the comforts of corporate headquarters and the false sense of security of strong division financial reports and ask the question, "What are you doing?"

Questions for Consideration

- Overall, do you feel that employees in your organization feel appreciated?

- Do you feel appreciated?

- Do you feel that your spouse, children, and loved ones feel valued?

- Are employees appropriately rewarded in your organization?

- Specifically, what improvements could be made in your company that would assist others in seeing the cathedral?

- At what stage do you see your family cathedral (Form, Storm, Norm, or Perform)? What about your organizational cathedral?

TOOLS TO BUILD YOUR CATHEDRAL

CHAPTER TWENTY-FOUR

Be Good in Addition to Being Great

IT HAS BEEN SAID THAT AMERICA is great because she is first good. In the bestseller *Good to Great*, the author suggests that truly "great" companies were first "good" companies. The CEOs of these "good to great" companies are not flashy and flamboyant. In fact, the CEOs are more like Christopher Wren, modest and simple. They don't have huge egos or think everything revolves around them.

In the book, *Short of the Glory*, the late Ed Pritchard of Kentucky was quoted as saying, "Great men are seldom good men." Prichard was a brilliant attorney who, as a young man, left home to work in the Roosevelt administration. He later came back to Kentucky, where he broke an election law, was convicted, and spent time in federal prison. While his later years were productive and devoted to educational reform, much of his early life was destructive, both personally and professionally. Pritchard's words have both haunted and motivated me throughout my life. "Cathedral" builders do not build Cathedrals at the expense of their families, or at the expense of being good.

In the brilliant movie *Saving Private Ryan*, an old James Ryan returns with his family to the military cemetery in Normandy. He visits the grave of Captain John Miller, the man who, a half a century before, led the mission to save Private Ryan. At the end of the mission, Miller was fatally wounded. As he lay dying, his final words to Private Ryan were, "James. Earn this...earn it." We then see Ryan kneeling at Captain Miller's grave, marked by a cross. Ryan, his voice trembling with emotion, says, "Every day I think about what you said to me that day on the bridge. I tried to live my life the best that I could. I hope that was enough. I hope that, at least in your eyes, I've earned what all of you have done for me."

Weeping, Ryan turns to his wife and says, "Tell me I've led a good life...tell me I am a good man."

Confused, she responds, "What?"

Choked up, he manages to make a second request. "Tell me I'm a good man."

Her response, like this entire scene, chokes me up: "You are."

Questions for Consideration

- How can you use your "good" to build a "great" Cathedral?
- What would others say about your "good"?
- Does Ryan's question provoke you to want to build a better life?
- Is your organization great because it is first good?
- What about you personally? You and I may be considered great because of what we've accomplished in our careers, but are we good?
- What changes do you need to make to bring about more good?

CHAPTER TWENTY-FIVE

Laugh, Think, and Cry

MOST OF US CAN REMEMBER what has been called the greatest college basketball game of all time: the 1982 NCAA championship game that featured North Carolina State upsetting the favored University of Houston team. I personally will never forget Coach Jim Valvano running onto the court, all his players already paired up with another teammate, desperately looking for someone to embrace. That scene is in heavy rotation in the opening sequence for every NCAA tournament broadcast, but more importantly for me, and I'm sure for many others, is the feeling of wanting to jump through my TV and hug Coach Valvano. That scene has never left me. In fact, it has provided the inspiration and my personal goal to be sincerely happy for other's success as I was for Coach Valvano at the end of that game in 1982.

Ten years after that famous game and only a few months before losing his battle to cancer, Coach Valvano received the Arthur Ashe Humanitarian Award. And in front of thousands of supporters and millions of TV viewers, he challenged us to do three things every day. The following is an excerpt from that famous speech:

"To me, there are three things we all should do every day. We should do this every day of our lives. Number one is Laugh. You should laugh every day. Number two is Think. You should spend some time in thought. Number three is you should have your emotions moved to tears–could be happiness or joy. But think about it. If you Laugh, you Think, and you Cry, that's a full day. That's a heck of a day. You do that seven days a week, you're going to have something special."

The concept of Laugh and Think every day is easy to comprehend, and most would agree is "doable." But what about the Cry every day? Do we really want to cry every day? Jim Valvano didn't mean a sad cry as much as he meant what I describe as a Holy Spirit cry. If there is a part of the Holy Trinity that is both under-preached and misunderstood, it is the Holy Spirit. The Holy Spirit is "Christ within us," and if you've started to cry in church when that praise and worship song tugged at your heart, that's the Holy Spirit. If you see a father and a grown son embrace at a restaurant and you find yourself getting watery eyes, that's the Holy Spirit. Laugh, Think, and Cry every day.

Questions for Consideration

- Who in your life may be running around the court looking for someone to hug?

- How do you congratulate others when they are successful?

- Is there someone you need to call, visit or send a note of congratulations? Even a belated one could make a huge difference in someone's life.

- Do you Laugh, Think and Cry every day?

- Which one(s) are the hardest to do each day? Why?

- What do you think Valvano meant by "cry each day"?

Touch Others

MY GRANDMOTHER WAS A RESIDENT of a nursing home, and one day after a visit I found myself having difficulty finding my way out of this facility. As I turned the corner, visibly confused and disoriented, a young orderly took notice and came to my rescue. Frustrated, I asked, "Can you help me get out of here?"

"Walk with me," the young man said as he guided me through the labyrinth of hallways and corridors. Not, "Go down that hallway, take a left, a right, then another left."

As we navigated our way to the closest exit, numerous patients suffering from dementia were lined in the hallways, sitting in their wheelchairs unresponsive, heads down and completely unaware of our journey.

With the precision of a skilled surgeon, this young man placed his tender and loving hand on the shoulder of each patient he passed, creating a visible reaction in each person he touched. This young man, who I'm sure never attended a seminar or read a book on the power of touch, provided a dose of medicine more effective than any conventional treatment. He did this naturally, with love and compassion.

I am reminded of Luke 8:44-46, where the woman touches the garment of Jesus. "Who was it that touched me?" Jesus asks.

Peter responds, "There are many people around you."

Jesus continues, "Someone touched me, for I perceive the power has gone out of me." Just like the orderly at the nursing home, we too have the power to touch others when it originates from the heart, when it's sincere and full of love.

Questions for Consideration

- How does touching others strengthen the Cathedral Building process?
- Specifically, how do we touch others? How do we let others touch us?
- Is this difficult for you to do? Why or why not?
- How can organizations touch others?
- From a customer service perspective, is your organization one of "Walk with me" (like the orderly in the above story) or more one of, "You see that hallway down there? Take a left and then your first right..."?

Hug Others

I WAS IN MY CAR AT THE intersection, listening to talk radio go on and on about the horrible economy, the increasing unemployment rates, out-of-control spending and the federal debt. I was pretty low to say the least. I looked to my right and there were approximately ten young ladies all dressed in black with posters that read, "Free Hugs." I then focused on two mechanics running out of a garage and getting a hug from each one of these young ladies. Emotions overcame me and I began to cry. Remember Jim Valvono's challenge? (1) Laugh, (2) Think and (3) Have your emotions move you to tears.

As I switched from talk radio to my favorite 70s and 80s station, I moved my car to the next intersection. Again, I saw about the same number of young ladies dressed in black with posters that read, "Free Hugs." I blew my horn and they waved and screamed. I quickly put my car in park, walked out into the street, and received ten of the sweetest, warmest and most sincere hugs in the world! I cried again. Jimmy V would be proud!

The 20 young ladies I saw that day were an army of roughly 10,000 Paul Mitchell Salon students who take to the street every September 23rd throughout the United States and celebrate their nationwide "Free Hugs Day." The tradition was inspired by the "Sick Puppies" YouTube music video about Juan Mann's popular "Free Hugs" campaign.

"As members of the beauty industry, we're in the business of helping people look beautiful. More importantly, it's part of our 'Be Nice' culture to help people feel beautiful. Our Free Hugs campaign is just one of the many ways our future professionals show their passion and compassion in their local communities," says Winn Claybaugh, dean and cofounder of Paul Mitchell Schools.

A hug can no doubt break down barriers that sometimes words cannot, and at times a hug can speak more than any words can say. We bond with a hug. We find comfort with a hug. We greet and separate from each other with a hug. We establish human contact and interaction with a hug. The beauty of a hug may just be in its simplicity. The gesture toward another human being, known or unknown, is easy. It costs nothing but a simple act of caring and kindness.

Human beings thrive on touch and often languish without it. We are social creatures. The simple act of hugging can lift a person and make him or her feel connected to someone else. When you embrace another human being, for those few moments you have to let go of everything and focus on that hug. The world is often a cold and distant place, and we build walls around us to keep others at bay. In the process we often lose what is most important. We get caught up in battles to survive. We forget that we need to do more than just survive and exist. We need to live. This open and genuine gesture called a hug can, if only for a moment, break down the walls that often separate us. A hug can momentarily bring two people back to the most basic reason for being.

What separates us from machines is not our intelligence and reasoning. It is, instead, the ability to connect on a level that only a living, breathing being can feel and comprehend. The connection of touch and love is a basic need and part of ourselves that makes us flourish. At the same time it is an unexplainable, mysterious feeling that no other can replace. Touch is water to our roots. A hug is one source of the water that feeds us.

Questions for Consideration

- How can Cathedral Builders use hugging to build other Cathedrals?
- Do you hug enough?
- What keeps us from hugging more?
- Who in your life needs a hug today?
- How are you showing passion and compassion in the community? What about your organization?

Help Others Realize What They Do Matters and Makes a Difference

MY SON WORKED AT MCDONALD'S during high school, and occasionally I would stop on my way to work to say hello. One morning, while leaving that McDonald's parking lot, I saw a gentleman sweeping and picking up trash. Obviously, he didn't look too excited. As I passed, I rolled down my window and said, "Sir, I want to tell you how great this parking lot looks! My first impression of a restaurant is how clean the parking lot is and I can tell you, you are doing an excellent job!"

Initially stunned but eventually smiling, he said, "Thank you." I can still remember looking in the rearview mirror and noticing the pep in his step as he continued cleaning the parking lot.

That night my son asked, "Did you tell Scott how good the parking lot looked this morning?" When I answered in the affirmative, my son replied, "Dude, you made his day!"

A former boss of mine used to call each direct report on Christmas Eve and simply tell each of us how much we meant to him, what a difference we were making for the company, and in general how much he appreciated our friendship and commitment to the company. Naturally, I would have done anything for this man. It was the difference between commitment and compliance.

Managers seek compliance; leaders receive commitment. It was a simple but so very powerful gesture that created a culture of appreciation that paid both financial and emotional dividends. Interestingly, after that boss left our division for a big promotion at corporate, my wife exclaimed, "I miss John like a death!" Think about it. A leader that provided leadership and a personal touch that not only motivated the employee but also garnered the support and admiration of the employee's spouse! Very powerful.

Questions for Consideration

- How many people's day could you make by simply acknowledging the value they bring to your organization?

- How many people could you touch today? Really touch! What about that person who cleans your office? What about that employee in the back corner with whom no one associates? Maybe just simply going to his/her cubicle and spending a few minutes "shooting the breeze" could make a real difference.

- Have you considered calling your direct reports for no reason other than telling them how much you value and appreciate them?

CHAPTER TWENTY-SIX

Send Handwritten Notes

SOME CREDIT JIMMY CARTER'S successful run for governor of Georgia to his handwritten notes to everyone he met on the campaign trail. When he was campaigning, a staff member would follow behind the candidate and say to every person he met, "You just met Jimmy Carter and we think he's going to be the next governor of Georgia. We'd like to send you some information. Do you mind giving us your name and address?" The staff person would get the name of the entire family.

Each person received a handwritten note–"Dear Joel and Pam, you just met Jimmy Carter, hopefully the next governor or Georgia. We would appreciate your vote, so nice to see you, thank you very much." Signed: *Jimmy Carter*. A real signature, not an electronic one!

Handwritten notes make a real difference in creating brand loyalty, and cost very little money. I travel on a regular basis and have stayed in almost every hotel chain across the country, each having a goal of making my stay as comfortable as possible and hoping to create some level of loyalty in the process. In every hotel room, there is a standard feedback form asking a series of questions related to my stay. Were you satisfied with the check-in process? Were you satisfied with the cleanliness of your room? Quality of food? Amenities of the hotel? I can't ever recall taking the time to fill out one of these cards.

However, on a business trip to Missouri, I stayed at a Holiday Inn Express and was blown away as I checked into my third floor room. I had been on the road all week, missing my family, and exhausted from the day's work. As I opened my hotel room door, threw my suitcase on the bed, and made my way to the nightstand to plug my cell phone charger into the wall outlet, I noticed what looked like a small, inexpensive Thank You card. As I opened the card I was blown away with not only the simplicity of this customer service gesture, but also the sincerity that went into writing it. It was a handwritten note shown here.

> Hello! Thank you for taking the time to read this card. As your house keepers we would like to welcome you to 3rd floor. It is our goal to make sure your experience is a happy relaxing time. We want you to think of this room as your home away from home, not just another hotel room. If there is anything we can do to improve your stay please let us know. Thank-you for choosing the Holiday Inn Express. Enjoy your stay
> — Trudy + michelle

Which hotel created loyalty? The glitzy four-star hotel with the generic feedback form printed on the finest cardstock, or the Holiday Inn Express that empowered its house cleaning staff to make guests feel as comfortable as possible and find some personal and unique way to thank customers for their business?

I was on the board of a non-profit organization where we sent out several thousand letters requesting financial support. While the letter was a formal typed letter, each board member selected those they knew and/or with whom they had a personal connection and simply wrote a few lines to the right of the margin, making an otherwise formal, very impersonal letter significantly more personal. For instance, a letter addressed to Jim had a few handwritten lines that would say something like this: "Jim, thanks for all that you do and the leadership you provide our community. Thanks in advance for your support!" It was then signed on the margin by the one who had the relationship. Now, instead of some formal letter with a stamped signature from an unknown person, it is from a friend with whom it would be hard not to provide some amount of support. Writer's cramp after signing 1000 letters? Yes! Worth it? Yes! We doubled our fundraising goal!

Questions for Consideration

- Do you send personal, handwritten notes?
- What are your thoughts/reactions when you receive a personal, handwritten note?
- Do you have personal stationery?
- Who could you make a difference with if you simply wrote them a note?
- Which hotel is more like your organization?
- Specifically, how could your organization touch others?

Realize Everyone Needs a Present, Everyone Needs Attention

ONE YEAR I WAS ASKED to play Santa Claus for the residents at a nursing home. I agreed, not really knowing what to expect, as my previous experiences had been with younger children. The setup was basically the same with the exception of the roles having been reversed. Instead of the parents bringing the children to see Santa Claus, the residents' families, usually their children, facilitated the visit and gifts from Santa Claus. Now, I realize we leave this world the same way we enter, having someone take care of us and attending to our basic needs; however, I wasn't ready for what I was about to experience playing Santa Claus for the elderly.

The residents were as excited as young children, with many unresponsive patients suddenly coming alive when Santa Claus arrived. For most residents, it was as if Santa was an old friend they felt they should know but weren't quite sure who he was. And I responded as such. It wasn't the normal "Ho, Ho, Ho! Merry Christmas." It was more like, "Hey, how in the world have you been?"

Unfortunately, nursing homes are not just for the elderly. In one room was a young man who was in the final stages of a deteriorating disease and while he could see, he was almost 100% immobile and unresponsive. While Santa Claus loved on this young man, I couldn't help but notice his parents crying, as they remembered happier holidays when their son was home and well.

As Santa Claus wandered into the main living room area, I started handing out the presents family members had brought for the residents. A few elves who knew the residents' names would whisper, "This one is for Mr. Cornwell. He's sitting over there." I loved on every resident, and the warmth I felt was indeed a spiritual experience. As I was handing out the presents, I felt a tug on

Santa Claus's coat. It was an elderly lady who looked up at me with childlike eyes and sadly asked, "Where's my present?"

She was the only resident who did not have a present and no relatives present for this holiday celebration. And while the employees hustled and finally found her a token present, the wait was a painful one for her. The reality of what she must have felt while everyone else had stacks of presents and she had none continues to choke me up. We never get too old or too important for attention. And, we never outgrow the need for a present.

"For I was hungry and you gave me something to eat, I was thirsty and you gave me something to drink, I was a stranger and you invited me in, I needed clothes and you clothed me, I was sick and you looked after me, I was in prison and you came to visit me.' Then the righteous will answer him, 'Lord, when did we see you hungry and feed you, or thirsty and give you something to drink? When did we see you a stranger and invite you in, or needing clothes and clothe you? When did we see you sick or in prison and go to visit you?' The King will reply, 'Truly I tell you, whatever you did for one of the least of these brothers and sisters of mine, you did for me.'"

—Matthew 25:35-40

Questions for Consideration

- Who's tugging on your coat, needing your attention?
- What present do you need to deliver and to whom?
- Have you considered visiting a nursing home and spending time with someone who is lonely?
- What about serving as a Big Brother/Sister to a needy child?
- What about a prison ministry?
- Is there an individual and/or family you should adopt during the holidays?

Have a Yes Face

THERE IS AN INTRIGUING STORY about the third president of the United States, Thomas Jefferson. One day, President Jefferson and his entourage were traveling across the country on horseback. They came upon a river flooded over its banks and the bridge washed away. The decision was made to cross the river on horseback. Rider after rider plunged into the river. About this time, a stranger approached the president and asked if he could ride with him across the river. The commander-in-chief said yes without hesitation. After the man slid off the president's horse, safely on the other side of the river, one of the president's companions scolded the man, "Why did you ask the president for a ride across the river?"

The man looked at him and explained that he had no idea that he was the president then said, "Some people have a 'Yes Face,' and some people have a 'No Face.' He had a Yes Face."

Interestingly, research suggests that among listeners, only seven percent of meaning is derived from the actual words we use, 38 percent from the tone of our voice, with the remaining 55 percent of meaning being assumed from our nonverbals (our Yes or No Faces). I am amazed how frequently I enter a place of business where the faces of the associates say "No." In fact, many churches I've attended and been a member of have greeters who clearly have No Faces. And I must confess, I've been guilty. Our nonverbals indeed speak louder than our words.

Having a Yes Face is no doubt good business, but being able to read other's faces appears to be good business as well. A recent *USA Today* article (10-25-11) profiled a hotel that is tailoring its interaction with guests based on body language. Employees have gone through training focusing on what cues to look for in making the customer experience a more pleasant and memorable one. For instance, a customer who makes eye contact while walking down the hall may be more open for conversation. A guest who tugs on his/her ear could indicate stress and be more open to hearing about the hotel's yoga kit or a therapeutic pillow.

Think of the foundational story at the beginning of this book and what the nonverbals of each Bricklayer communicated to Christopher Wren. The first bricklayer was crouched, no eye contact, most likely communicating total disengagement. The second bricklayer, who could at least see the wall, was half-standing, communicating lack of confidence at the very minimum. But the third bricklayer's nonverbals communicated full engagement, confidence, and success as he exclaimed, "I'm building a Cathedral to The Almighty!"

I speak to school systems across the country and my challenge to students is to be a Cathedral Builder. Sit up front, show interest, develop a relationship with the teacher, and get involved in extracurricular activities.

Questions for Consideration

- Thinking about a Cathedral as a place that welcomes everyone, what can you do to create this environment?

- Does your face say, "Glad to meet you, I'm here to help," or does it say "Don't bother me. I'm too busy. I really don't want to talk."

- What does your face say to others? Do you have a Yes Face or a No Face? What are your nonverbals communicating?

- Listen to your voice mail. Does it communicate excitement, engagement?

- What is the general tone of your e-mails? Maybe a simple, "Thanks for your help!" versus, "Thank you for your quick attention to this matter" could make a big difference in your personal effectiveness and your Emotional Intelligence score.

- What about your company? Is it a "Yes" culture or a "No" culture?

- Does your company provide training on the "soft skills" of nonverbal communication or total focus on "technical training?" Which one creates customer loyalty?

Focus on The Almighty,
Not Those Who Are Persecuting You

ATLANTA-BASED TV MINISTER CHARLES STANLEY tells a story about a time in his ministry when he was struggling and experiencing lots of opposition and conflict. In the midst of this turmoil, an elderly member of his church invited him to her home. Stanley hesitated. It was a busy time, and he was reluctant to go. She insisted, and he finally gave in and visited this elderly woman. Upon entering her home, she said, "I want to show you something." She took him to her living room where hanging on the wall was a painting of Daniel in the Lion's den. She said, "Look at this painting and tell me what you see." Stanley looked at the painting and saw the lions, the bones on the floor, and many other features—but missed the most important aspect of this painting. After a few minutes, she put her arm around him and said, "What I want you to see is, Daniel doesn't have his eyes on the lions, but on Christ." Charles Stanley goes on to say that was the greatest message he could receive at that time in his life.

Questions for Consideration

- Overall, where is your current focus?
- Is it time to focus less on the "Lions" in your life?

Ask Others to Tell You Their Story

I WAS IN WASHINGTON, DC at the Hyatt Regency Hotel attending a conference when I saw a shoeshine stand. One of life's greatest pleasures, in my opinion, is getting one's shoes shined by a true professional. It is indeed a lost art. The sign at this particular shoeshine stand said, "Be back in 15 minutes." I had some free time so I waited. Within a few minutes, a very professional-looking man entered a small area near the men's restroom, removed his overcoat and asked, "Are you ready for a shoeshine, Sir?" A little surprised, I jumped up on the chair and let the man who looked like a United States senator do his magic.

Now, I could have let this gentleman shine my shoes while I read my *USA Today*, paid the $6, and gone about my day. Then, I would not only have missed an opportunity to help someone realize how he was building Cathedrals (although I'm quite sure he was well aware of what he was building); I would have missed an opportunity to be inspired and motivated by this man's story. I couldn't resist asking this artist, "Would you tell me your story?"

He told the story of growing up in New York and starting to shine shoes at the airport as a teenager. He was recruited by the FBI later moving to Washington, DC. He continued moonlighting and shining shoes on the side, where he touched and inspired some of the most important and powerful people in the world. He eventually left the FBI because they had him "laying bricks" behind a desk instead of building a Cathedral. He continues to shine shoes today, demonstrating how Cathedrals indeed come in many shapes and many forms.

Everyone has a story to tell and, for the most part, want to be asked and take great pride and joy in telling their story. Don't miss the opportunity to inspire others, learn from others, sharpen your listening skills, show the deepest respect ever, and all by simply asking others to tell you their story. And, be open to and not afraid to tell others your story!

Questions for Consideration

- How can you provide a platform for others to share their story?

- How can you ensure others know that you have an attentive ear?

- Do you ask others to tell their story?

- Are you too busy to ask and/or too busy telling your story?

- Do you feel comfortable telling your story? If used appropriately, this form of self-disclosure builds trust.

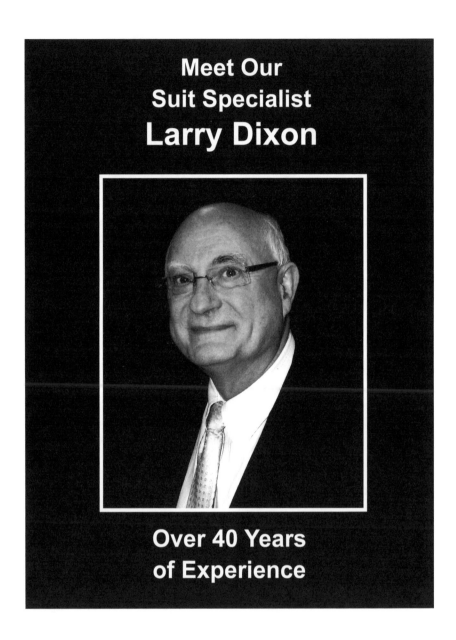

CHAPTER TWENTY-SEVEN

Recognize Greatness

LIKE MOST SMALL TOWNS many years ago, my hometown had a clothing store where the local owner would greet you as you walked in the door and whatever your financial status, treated you and your family like royalty. While the suit-clad local bank president was responsible for me wanting to be a "businessman," Larry Dixon was responsible for me wanting to be in sales. He was the motivation for me to use my vocation to touch and inspire others, the motivation for me wanting to be "good." Larry Dixon was and continues to be a legend, not only in our hometown, but also across the region and now within Dillard's, the Fortune 500 company where he works. Larry Dixon owned Sullivan's department store in Franklin, Kentucky, my hometown. And while my family was never responsible for any sales records being broken, the times we did enter his store, he made us feel like we were his top customers. I can hear him like it was yesterday asking my parents about a family member, "Bill and Barbara, tell me, how is Nell doing?" In the truest sence, Larry Dixon was a Cathedral Builder. He didn't sell clothes; he sold memories. He wasn't driven by profits; he was driven by touching and inspiring others.

Downtown merchants have always been pillars of commerce in small towns, but the Walmart's of the world, the mega malls and online shopping have dealt them a serious blow. Like the owners of thousands of local stores across small-town America,

Larry Dixon would eventually be forced to close the doors of his downtown Cathedral. Larry Dixon could have gone home and cursed the Walmarts and the mall department stores, and no one would have blamed him. But that's not Larry Dixon's character. As a master craftsman, he still had the drive and passion to build Cathedrals. Larry Dixon's Cathedral wasn't narrowly focused on simply Sullivan's department store; his Cathedral was much broader. His Cathedral was, and is to this day, to use his vocation to touch others in a deep and meaningful way. He wants to make people feel their very best or, in his words, "To be a Christian example to all of whom I come in contact."

And just like London after the fire of 1666, Larry Dixon experienced his own form of devastation. After building a business from the ground up, pouring out his heart and soul, he would eventually be forced to close its doors. But after the smoke cleared, Larry Dixon knew he had to persevere, as there were more Cathedrals to be built.

Within a matter of months, Dillard's called the master craftsman to assist them in building and branding its Cathedral. Predictably, it wasn't long until Larry Dixon was not only breaking all sales records, he was also building the loyalty that all retail outlets strive to achieve. Customers were not the only ones starting to notice new levels of service; the Christopher Wren at corporate headquarters, who just happened to be the son of the founder and the namesake for the company, started to notice the significant increase in sales.

The president of Dillard's picked up the phone and called the regional manager, who then called the store manager and asked the question, "Who is Larry Dixon?" After the store manager told the "Larry Dixon" story, the company president, the "Christopher Wren of corporate America," arranged a trip to Bowling Green to meet the master craftsman. The company president understood Bricklayers don't build customer loyalty any more than managers who scream monthly sales targets across showroom floors inspire or motivate associates. Cathedral Builders don't sell suits; they sell memories. It is the Christopher Wren who gets out from behind his or her desk and asks the question, "What are you doing?" that reminds associates they're not selling suits; they're increasing the likelihood of that young man landing that first job because he knows how great he looks and projects that feel and confidence during the interview.

And while any customer who meets Larry Dixon quickly realizes he is dealing with a true Cathedral Builder, the company president didn't want to leave anything to chance. "Larry, our customers need to know of your experience and our commitment to superior customer service." And while most corporate bureaucrats would have found 100 reasons why not to recognize a Cathedral Builder ("If we do it for him, we'll have to do it for everybody"), this Christopher Wren was determined to think outside the box and do something beautiful. If you visit Dillard's in Bowling Green, Kentucky, you will see a photo of Larry Dixon on the showroom floor with the words, "Meet Our Suit Specialist Larry Dixon. Over 40 Years of Experience."

Questions for Consideration

- What Cathedral Building characteristics did Larry have that are worthy of emulating when you are thrust into unforeseen and difficult situations?

- Who are the people who have made a difference in your life? That fundamentally shaped your thinking?

- Have you told them what a difference they've made in your life? If not, why?

- What keeps us from reaching out and telling those who have made a difference in our lives?

- Does your organization celebrate greatness? If not, why? How could it do a better job of celebrating greatness?

CHAPTER TWENTY-EIGHT

Never Underestimate the Amazing Power and Responsibility of Being a Leader

WHEN THE PEOPLE YOU SUPERVISE go home for the day, who do you think they're talking about over the dinner table? Most likely, it's not the CEO of your company. It's probably not even a senior manager within your company. If you have direct reports, they're talking about you more than you probably realize. How you treat them impacts them not only at work, but also influences their entire life! What an amazing responsibility and power we have with the people with whom we work. And it goes much further than simply a direct report's immediate family. I was having dinner with a friend and asked about his older brother. My friend responded, "We're really worried about Steve. His boss is horrible and it's literally killing him." Wow! So, this one toxic manager is negatively impacting a direct report, his spouse and children, his brother, and many others who are concerned and worried about his situation. Never underestimate the power and responsibility of being a leader. Leadership is not an option! Manage the business, but lead your people.

Questions for Consideration

> • What are your direct reports saying about you over the dinner table?
>
> • As a leader, are you a source of motivation or a source of stress?

Seek Significance

IN BOB BUFORD'S BESTSELLING BOOK, *HALFTIME*, he uses the metaphor of a football game. He suggests that the "first half" of our lives, we don't think too much about how we will spend the rest of our lives. We rush through college, get married, start a career, climb the corporate ladder, and buy lots of toys. At some point in our lives, however, we start to wonder if this is as good as it gets. Somehow, keeping score does not offer the thrill it once did. Buford admits that during the first half, we take some vicious hits and often suffer personal fires, such as divorce, too much alcohol, guilt, not spending enough time with our children, or loneliness.

Like many good players, Buford suggests we start the "second half" with good intentions but get blindsided along the way. While the first half was about success, the second half for many is about significance. The game is won or lost in the second half, not the first. Some people never get to the second half, as the prevailing view in our society is that once you reach your mid-forties, you enter a period of aging and decline. Buford challenges us to discredit the view that the second half of our lives will never measure up to the first, and make the transition from success to significance.

Questions for Consideration

- What turning points have you had in your life that have improved your focus for seeking significance?
- What is the focus in your life: Success or Significance?
- Are you happy with this focus?
- If not, what specific steps do you need to take?

That Which Is Essential Is Invisible to the Eye

I THINK WE ALL WOULD AGREE we tend to lose sight of what's really important in life. Unfortunately, the death of a loved one usually brings us all back to reality. What is really important in life? It's not our house that's three times larger than the house in which we grew up. It's not even our car that costs more than the house in which we grew up. The most important things in life are the intangibles. "That which is essential is invisible to the eye," was something that I learned as a Sigma Chi fraternity pledge some 30 years ago.

The value of the simple things in life was brought into focus when my grandfather passed away. He was a simple, "salt of the earth" man born, raised and having died in the hills of Tennessee. I received word from my dad that my grandfather had died. "Greg, your granddad died today, and he would like to be buried in the overalls you gave him." I purchased those overalls in connection with an event many years ago that had a "hillbilly" theme. Realizing that I would never wear them again, I had given them to my dad who in turn gave them to my grandfather.

I assumed my grandfather had worn those overalls on a regular basis, wearing them out, and eventually discarding them. I was wrong. My grandfather viewed those overalls as I would have viewed a brand-new suit. He only wore them to town on Saturday and on special occasions. Minutes before he died, he had asked to be buried in those "overalls that Greg gave me." My grandfather was buried in a wooden casket in a family cemetery on top of a mountain in Tennessee. With just a handful of family members on a rainy, dreary, foggy day, my cousin Johnny played his banjo to a country hymn and, "that which was essential, was clearly visible to the eye."

Questions for Consideration

- Have you, like most, made your life way too complex? Why?
- Specifically, what steps do you need to take to simplify?
- Has a personal Fire caused you to refocus?

CHAPTER TWENTY-NINE

Forgive and Reconcile

I FIRST MET DAN CHERRY when he was Secretary of the Kentucky Justice Cabinet. I had conducted a team-building workshop for then Governor Paul Patton and his executive cabinet. Like most heroes, you would have never known of this legend by his quiet demeanor and humble spirit. But it didn't take long to realize Dan Cherry was, and is to this day, an amazing man; he is a Cathedral Builder.

Brigadier General Dan Cherry, USAF (Ret.) served our country for 29 years, flying airplanes such as the F-105, the F-4 and the F-16. He also commanded the Air Force Thunderbirds, the 8th Tactical Fighter Wing and the Air Force Recruiting Service. Dan Cherry is indeed one of many specialized craftsmen continuing to build a Cathedral that started in 1776, when America claimed independence from England. That Cathedral is still being built today by the over one million brave men and women serving in our armed services.

On April 16, 1972, then Major Dan Cherry was on a mission near Hanoi, North Vietnam when he encountered a dogfight that would change his life. Major Cherry squeezed the trigger of his radar-guided AIM-7 Sparrow missile, hitting a North Vietnamese MiG-21 jet, which exploded in a huge fireball. The MiG pilot ejected, and his parachute opened directly in front of Major Cherry.

Dan Cherry continued to serve his country many years after that eventful day over North Vietnam and, like most Cathedral Builders, he found many other Cathedrals that needed his well-honed skills, his passion and sense of purpose.

Just like the Cathedrals built hundreds of years ago, modern-day Cathedrals need someone like Dan Cherry who not only see the need for such a monument, but is willing to provide the leadership, the passion, and the perseverance to see it to completion. Such was the case with Dan Cherry's dream of the Aviation Heritage Park in Bowling Green, Kentucky. But little did Dan Cherry realize this particular Cathedral would change his life and the lives of many others in ways no one could have ever imagined. And that's the beauty of Cathedrals. When we pursue our passions, we usually find that in addition to our lives being forever altered, others' lives will be significantly changed as well.

Dan Cherry and a group of his walking buddies from Bowling Green took a trip to the National Museum of the United States Air Force in Dayton, Ohio. The one exhibit that changed lives that day wasn't even at the museum. Knowing that Dan Cherry and his friends were from Kentucky, a staff member commented about an airplane that held some historical significance to the Bluegrass State. He told them it might become available because the VFW where it was located was having difficultly taking care of it. As fate would have it, that VFW was only 20 miles down the road. To the group's amazement, the number 66-7550 on the tail of the F-4 Phantom jet left no doubt that Major Dan Cherry had been reunited with an old friend from 30 years earlier.

Dan Cherry's F-4 Phantom jet soon had a new home in Bowling Green, and it became clear that the seed of an idea planted with the discovery of that plane had flowered into something much bigger than anyone had ever imagined. And while a Cathedral is never completed, today the Aviation Heritage Park honors some of America's finest combat aviators, with plans to host many more airplanes and honor the pilots who flew these magnificent machines.

Cathedrals have many purposes. They are a place of worship. They are a place for introspection. They very often leave us with more questions about who we are than when we entered. The Aviation Heritage Park played such a role for Dan Cherry. "For over 30 years, I filed away memories of that MiG pilot that I shot down," recalls Dan Cherry. "Did he have a family? Did he survive the bailout and return to fly again?" Curious, Dan Cherry wrote a letter to a journalist and TV show anchor in Vietnam, and only a few weeks later, Dan Cherry received an invitation to appear on the show *The Separation Never Seems to Have Existed.*

Thirty years after that life-changing dogfight, Dan Cherry would meet Nyugen Hong My, the pilot of the defeated MiG-1. Since then, the two men have become close friends, spending time together both in Vietnam and in the United States. The power of forgiveness and reconciliation prompted Nyugen Hong My to ask Dan Cherry to research the American pilot that the Vietnamese pilot had shot down. Dan Cherry kept his promise, and on April 26, 2009, Nyugen Hong My and the American he shot down embraced each other with tears in their eyes as Steve Hartman of CBS News expressed, "The war went away."

Dan Cherry went on to write *My Enemy, My Friend* that is a must read. Proceeds from the sale of his book go to the Aviation Heritage Park in Bowling Green, Kentucky. To purchase your copy, visit their website at www.aviationheritagepark.com today.

Questions for Consideration

- What leadership skills could be learned from Dan Cherry and Nyugen Hong My that are essential in building Cathedrals?
- Is there someone needing your forgiveness?
- Is there someone with whom you need to reconcile?
- Could you perhaps be a catalyst, a facilitator in helping others start the forgiveness and reconciliation process?
- What action steps are necessary to accomplish the above?

"First be reconciled to your brother, and then come and offer your gift."

—Matthew 5:24

DEVELOPING A "LIFE OF PURPOSE"

CHAPTER THIRTY

A Life of Purpose
Terry Curtis Daniels

AS I REFLECT ON MY LIFE and my pursuit of a "Life of Purpose," I see the unfolding of a life that had very humble beginnings. I grew up in a poor environment, in a family with no college graduates, with parents who didn't complete high school, and in an era that minimized the value of other races to say the least. What I wanted most was a "Life of Purpose." Unfortunately, my life had numerous obstacles that threatened my purpose. I wandered aimlessly through high school, eventually landing a factory job after graduation. Because of this wandering and lack of purpose, in my late teens and early twenties I became lost in drugs and alcohol. While I eventually enrolled at a local college, the lack of support from home and my lack of passion would make this first attempt short-lived. I started another factory job working swing shift and after a few years on the job discovered the company had an attractive tuition reimbursement program—a "Cathedral Building" program, if you will. The challenge of working swing shift and attending college was a huge undertaking, but a Life of Purpose was the motivation that kept me going.

After four years of factory work and attending college part-time, I accepted a call into the ministry. While the task of meeting multiple commitments was indeed challenging, the desire for a life of purpose provided both the drive and the energy to see me through. And while getting my degree took substantially longer than expected, I stayed committed. I was a Cathedral and I was building a Cathedral. A major source of my strength was my soon-to-be wife, Rita. We married and started a family, all while I was working a swing shift, pastoring a church, and attending college. For almost 20 years, I have been the pastor of the Loving Chapel Baptist Church in Franklin, Kentucky. During my ministry, we've had multiple building projects and moderate growth for a small rural church. Loving Chapel is indeed a Cathedral, and I am simply a caretaker. And the caretaker had a bout with prostate cancer but The Master Builder, God, cured me and I am now cancer free!

We are a rural, many would say country, church that has always struggled financially. The ability of the church to compensate me has been a challenge, often at the point of no compensation at all but both the church and I see our mission much bigger than ourselves. In addition to the ministry, I've worked for several Fortune 500 companies as a human resource manager, training and development leader, consultant, leader developer, and change agent. My work has required extensive travel, with me often returning home only to have to jump back in the car, supporting my children as they pursued their passions hundreds of miles down the road. In the midst of this and at the age of 48, I embarked upon a masters degree all while supporting my lovely wife Rita with her career goals and a Rank 1 certification in education.

I share my story as simply an illustration of how I've practiced and continue to practice the five steps to pursuing a life of purpose that follows. Do I think I am there? I can't answer that for sure, but I can say I am a Cathedral and a Cathedral Builder. If you involve yourself in something that supports and helps others, you are well on your way to developing a life of purpose. As I have found in scripture from The Master Builder, "He that loses his life shall find it" (Matthew 10:39). I am indeed finding a life of purpose in losing my life to the betterment of others.

Developing a Life of Purpose

Many people often ask the question, "How do I find my purpose?" or "What is my purpose?" I believe that's the wrong question. If you ask the wrong question, you may get an answer or answers that could lead you the wrong way for longer than planned. In a recent survey by Lifeway Research (2011), approximately 75% of the 2000 adults surveyed nationally indicated they either agreed or strongly agreed with the statement, "There is an ultimate purpose and plan for every person's life." Additionally, 78% agreed with the statement, "It is important that I pursue a higher purpose and meaning in life," while 67% agreed with the statement, "A major priority in my life is finding a deeper purpose." From the survey it's clear: most of us are indeed searching for purpose in our lives.

Maybe a more appropriate question should be, "How do I develop a life of purpose?" As evidenced by each story in this book, purpose cannot be confined to the singular. It has to be focused in a very pluralistic approach. Throughout this book, I've discovered several things about purpose that's important to understand before beginning the quest in developing one's life's purpose. As you view yourself and become a Cathedral, you must have a passion to become a Cathedral Builder. There are several things to remember about purpose:

- Purpose doesn't drain energy; it sustains energy–A person with a life of purpose receives his or her energy from the intrinsic desire to accomplish things far greater than an individual's skills and ability would logically dictate.

- Purpose isn't a burden; it's a pleasure – A person with a life of purpose views tasks and challenges as opportunities to build up others. He or she longs for and seeks these opportunities.

- Purpose isn't selfish; it's selfless – A person with a life of purpose consistently has eyes open looking for opportunities to support the betterment of others.

- Purpose doesn't steal joy; it restores joy – A person with a life of purpose is never depleted of inner joy. He or she is constantly excited by the gift to support the betterment of others.

- Purpose doesn't try to undo; it tries to renew – A person with a life of purpose doesn't spend time trying to undo life events and challenges, he or she accepts the hand dealt and build from there.

- Purpose doesn't measure impact; it just impacts – A person with a life of purpose doesn't measure his or her impact in scope and size, but in renewed joy, renewed strength, and renewed energy in others.

- Purpose isn't sought after; it's thrust upon – A person with a life of purpose doesn't seek purpose; purpose seeks him or her through life circumstances.

- Purpose isn't emotionally driven; its consistently realistic – A person with a life of purpose doesn't derive purpose out of an emotional event, he or she views events from a realistic point of view and responds as a matter of fact, not simply through emotion. Emotion tends to have a short life span in its effort to sustain long-term purpose.

A life with purpose is an amazing life to live. The question worth pursuing is "How do you develop a life of purpose?" While my step-by-step approach may be a simplified model, the answers actually originate from the many examples of purpose from the many ordinary people we've met in the pages of this book. There are also many other examples of purpose in the people you meet in your everyday life. As a pastor, father, husband, human resource manager, leader, and many other roles that I've played over the past 25 years, there are so many people that have taught, demonstrated, and allowed me to observe what a life of purpose looks like. People of purpose come from all walks of life; they don't have any particular credentials, status in society, name recognition, or any other measure that only serves to divide people. In short, we all have the capacity for a life of purpose. The question still remains, "How do we develop a life of purpose?

The following five steps, all taken from the examples in this book, will hopefully assist you in finding your life purpose. (Remember, you do not find purpose–purpose finds you while you are in the activities you choose to pursue).

1) *Get Involved* - Identify activities that benefit others and that put you in contact with like-minded people who are pursuing the betterment of others. In the story, "Free Hugs," several young women joined together to give free hugs as a way to show others they are valued, to simply make them feel good. While some may have taken advantage of the giving nature and good intentions of these young women, this was not on the minds of these young women and it cannot be on the minds of people of purpose. Some examples are:

a) Religious affiliation and involvement

b) Volunteer coaching young children in sports, dance, music, etc.

c) Caring for or visiting the elderly (even a more rich experience if you're not related)

d) Teaching Sunday school, Bible school, etc.

e) Volunteering to support local school activities (even a more rich experience if you don't have children at the school)

f) Community involvement (Big Brothers/Big Sisters, United Way, pregnancy crisis centers, etc.)

Whatever activities you get involved with, do it for pleasure and not measure. Some questions to consider when choosing and/or considering activities:

- If I were in the position of those I want to support, how would I feel about the help from others?

- If your answer to the above question is positive, then you should participate. Your life of purpose could easily be found in these activities.

- Do I have the time to consistently commit for a defined period of time?

- Will the activities stretch my skills, abilities, and faith? Hopefully, your response will be "Yes, a life of purpose is always bigger than the person."

2) *Become a Learner and Teach Others* - Endeavor and have a passion to learn, develop, and grow in your skills, knowledge, and abilities in the activities you have selected that have the greatest impact on others. In the story, "Recognize Greatness," Larry Dixon is a Cathedral and a Cathedral Builder because he is always in pursuit of learning and helping others. He lives the philosophy, "I don't sell suits; I sell memories." The learning can be formal or as informal as perfecting a bounce pass or the correct way to hold a musical instrument. Some examples would be:

a) Host a one-time group session to discuss how others have succeeded in similar activities.

b) Conduct research for information on a particular activity sharing with others as needed.

c) Ask people impacted the most what would benefit them. Share with others.

d) Early on, be a jack of all trades, eventually mastering one – one that ignites your passion. Congratulations! You're on your way to a life of purpose!

Again, whatever learning and development you pursue, do it for pleasure and not measure. Some questions to ask when choosing and/or considering learning options:

- If I were in the position of those I want to support, what would I want that person to know?

- In this activity, what do I know and what do I need to know to be effective? Is the learning a source of excitement? Will it be enjoyable?

- Do I have the time to consistently commit to the learning needed to make a difference?

- Am I willing and committed to make a real difference?

3) *Develop a Higher Vision* – In your chosen activities, develop a view that stretches your spiritual, mental, or physical abilities. In "Building a Cathedral to the Almighty," professional golfer Kenny Perry is a great golfer, but he has obviously linked those skills and abilities with a greater purpose. As a result, his vision is enlarged and becomes bigger than he is. The following are some examples:

a) Think outside the box of the potential benefits that could result from your activities.

b) Of those potential benefits, which excite you the most?

c) What are the potential benefits outside your sphere of influence? Your community?

d) How can you share these benefits with others? (Facebook group?)

Some questions to ask when developing your vision:

- If I were in the position of those I want to support, what vision would I want the person helping me to have?

- Does my perceived limited ability actually limit my ability to think of greater visions?

- Who are some people that have gone from rags to riches who were driven by purpose? (Oprah Winfrey, for example)

- Try this exercise: Imagine a billboard profiling the vision for your activity. Draw a picture of this vision including you next to the billboard. Hint: You should be very small!

4) *Celebrate Successes* – Be excited for the successes of others, even if you have to celebrate alone. In the story, "Laugh, Think, and Cry," Jim Valvano ran around the court looking for someone to hug as he celebrated the outcome of the game. Sometimes in life, we too have to celebrate alone. Naturally, there is that tug to simply sigh a little, "That was a good game" when perhaps the better response would be to jump for joy as Jim Valvano did. Maybe "jumping for joy" is making that phone call and offering a congratulations or writing that note that would certainly be a welcome correspondence days after the event. Be known for something that others take

for granted. Be known for making a difference! Some examples are:

a) Be a visible expression of commitment to helping others in your daily walk by recognizing and celebrating the smallest of achievements.

b) Consistently smile and encourage others daily, even if you get nothing in return.

c) Remember important dates of other people and send cards, e-mails, texts, or other efforts to show you're thinking of them (birthdays, anniversary, etc.).

d) If you remember the boss on Boss' Day, remember the administrative assistant on his or her day (no big "I"s or little "u"s).

Some questions to ask when identifying successes to celebrate:

- If I were in the position of those I want to support, what would I want to celebrate? (What's worth celebrating to one person may be different for another.)

- What's a big accomplishment for those in an activity in which you're involved?

- What can I do to encourage other supporters? Is there anyone that I could give a gift card to for his or her extra effort? (Not every celebration has to be public to have impact.)

- Establish some personal and group goals that you want to keep in front of you and/or the group.

5) *Leave a Lasting Legacy* - Provide foundations for other to build upon. It may just be your children, but it can be lasting. In "Forgive and Reconcile," the career and bravery of Dan Cherry continue to be an example of an

individual who has left an impact on all who have known him. Dan Cherry is indeed a Cathedral and Cathedral Builder. Dr. Martin Luther King, Jr. quoted the words to a Southern gospel song in one of his speeches, saying, "If I do my duty as a Christian ought; to bring salvation (deliverance) to a world once wrought, then my living will not be in vain." (Interestingly, one of the gospel groups that was renowned for performing this hymn was the Cathedral Quartet.)

Some examples would be:

a) Volunteer to do some of the simple things to help your group or community.

b) If you have a specialized skill and/or name recognition, use it to bring others on board.

c) Offer measurable and tangible benefits to others. "If you give a person a fish, he will eat for a day, but if you teach him to fish, he can eat for a lifetime."

d) Don't be the source; be the resource. Learn the resources at your disposal and then connect them for others.

Some questions to ask when developing a legacy:

• If I were in the position of those I want to support, what would leave a lasting impression on me?

• What do I do well, and what am I known for? Upon what is my current reputation based?

• What can I do in my daily walk to put a smile on the face of others?

- In one sentence, what would I want to be the title of my eulogy, or the epitaph on my tombstone?

Congratulations! You've made important steps in developing a life of purpose. The pursuit will provide as much or maybe more gratification than reaching your final destination. That final destination may never be met, but your pursuit will benefit millions!

CONCLUSION

CHAPTER THIRTY-ONE

Conclusion

IN THE DEVOTIONAL BOOK, *OUR DAILY BREAD*, Joe Stoewell, former president of Moody Bible Institute and current president of Cornerstone University in Grand Rapids, Michigan, suggests we too are like the great cathedrals of Europe, with buttresses of external influences holding us up while we remain weak at the core (*Our Daily Bread*, Discovery House Publishers, August 25, 2011). He goes on to suggest our current day buttresses come in many forms: pastors, friends, family, small groups, work associates. As "cathedrals", we start out as simply a dream in our parents' eyes, and through the vision and hard work of many people, we take shape and provide the inspiration for those external buttresses around us to continue the hard work and dedication needed to see a lifelong project to fruition.

In fact, many of those who support us over the years may never see our full potential, as they will pass on before the Cathedral is completed. But just as the walls and stained glass of the great cathedrals in Europe reflect the master craftsmen who built them, we too reflect the love and dedication of our grandparents, that elderly neighbor, that schoolteacher, that bus driver, that coach, and that pastor, giving thanks to the work, sweat and tears these artisans poured into our lives.

In Bill Shore's book, *The Cathedral Within*, he describes Cathedral Builders as most likely not considering inspiration and faith as simple byproducts of their work; it is their core purpose. Leadership was put to test every day and every year, motivating and inspiring scores of workers over the span of several hundred years to bring completion to the cathedral. In fact, most workers realized they would never live to see their final achievement. Shore outlines five fundamental principles of Cathedral Builders that give meaning and purpose to our lives:

(1) Your craftsmanship and dedication is not diminished by devoting your life to a cause you will never see completed.

(2) Building Cathedrals requires the sharing of strength and the contribution of not just the artisans and experts, but also of everyone in the community.

(3) Great Cathedrals are built upon the foundations of earlier efforts.

(4) Cathedrals were sustained and maintained because they actually generated their own wealth and support.

(5) Cathedrals, through their stained glass panels, statues, and paintings, were intentionally designed to convey stories and values to others.

And while a cathedral is both an architectural marvel and a shrine to human experience, it seems that the greatness of the cathedral is that it is a vast metaphor for humanity: diverse but striving toward harmony, grand but imperfect, and always a work in progress.

So we ask once more:

• How would you describe a Cathedral?

• Do you see yourself as a Cathedral?

• What are your personal Cathedrals?

- Are you actively pursuing these Cathedrals with passion and purpose?

- What steps do you need to take in building your Cathedrals?

- Do you see your job as a Cathedral?

- Do you think your employees/team members see their job as a Cathedral?

- What specifically could be done to create a Cathedral Builder culture in your organization?

While a Cathedral is a powerful metaphor, we have introduced others in this book that hopefully have provided meaning, understanding, and purpose in our lives. Captain Plumb's Parachute Packer is a catalyst for introspection for those who have made a difference in our lives. Specifically, who are they for you? Have you let them know what an impact they've had in your life? Is it time to pick up the phone and call them? Maybe send a note? Better yet, maybe a visit, a lunch.

The Bricklayers in the story invite us to ask which one we are most like. Maybe at work we view ourselves as building a Cathedral but at home are we simply going through the motions (or vice/versa)? And what would others say is our Cathedral?" Is it where we spend our most time? I revealed my Cathedral to my family one day as I exclaimed, "My goal this year is to get my handicap in the single digits." Only now do I realize why they looked at me like I was crazy. My "little c" (golf) was causing my "big C" (family) to crumble. My handicap is now the highest it's been while my family life is the best it's ever been!

We all have personal fires in our lives, but London hopefully provides inspiration to rebuild and become even greater than before. Rats and fleas were the major cause of the plaque that killed 10,000 people annually before the Great Fire of 1666. After the fire, the rats and fleas were eradicated. What are your "rats and fleas" that perhaps after a fire would be gone? Hatred? Pride? Resentment? Addiction? Maybe fire is the label, the metaphor we need to start the healing.

I am amazed that most Americans, other than architects, have never heard of Christopher Wren. What an amazing person! I am awed by his accomplishments, his modesty, his diversity, his adversity, his leadership. I am also amazed at how few people have actually heard of the parable of the "Bricklayers and the Cathedral Builder." And whether Christopher Wren actually asked those three bricklayers, "What are you doing?" getting the response, "I'm building a Cathedral to The Almighty" is a moot point if we use this story as a source of reflection, a source of discussion, and a catalyst for transformation.

Our goals for writing this book were really quite simple:

(1) To encourage you to never ever underestimate the power and the responsibility to touch others in a deep and meaningful way. No matter what your job is, what position you hold in your company, you have the power and responsibility to touch others.

(2) To realize whatever job you do, you determine if it's Laying Bricks or Building Cathedrals. To realize we all have the amazing power and responsibility to help others understand what they do is important and that they too are Building Cathedrals. To challenge you not to be dragged down by the Bricklayers in your life. To motivate you to break away from those who are having a negative influence in your life.

(3) To share real-life specific examples of how others have come out of Fires, the characteristics of those folks and how they're now Building Cathedrals.

(4) To encourage you to start writing your book today! Your stories are worth preserving and should be shared with others.

(5) To encourage you if you've not yet found your Cathedral, start looking! If you've found it but not started building it, start building! If you've started but lack the passion, get passionate!

(6) To reinforce the importance of supporting and encouraging others in building their Cathedrals.

(7) And, in the words of both Winston Churchill and Jim Valvano, "Never give up! Never, ever, ever, ever give up!"

So what does the future hold? While no one really knows for sure, the Cathedral Builders in our lives certainly provide the inspiration, motivation and vision to look to the future rather than looking back and focusing on our personal and societal "Fires." My friend, David Garvin, founder of Camping World and the epitome of a Cathedral Builder, having started, built and provided the vision for numerous business ventures, shared his economic predictions for the future with me just a few short weeks before the completion of this book. As I sat in his office, he made eight predictions for 2012, the very same predictions he's made since 1990 and ones that have made David Garvin one of the country's most successful leaders and entrepreneurs.

(1) Business will continue to go where invited and remain where appreciated.

(2) Reputations will continue to be made by many acts and lost by only one.

(3) People will continue to prefer doing business with friends.

(4) Performance will continue to outsell promises.

(5) Enthusiasm will be as contagious as ever.

(6) Know-how will surpass guess-how.

(7) Trust, not tricks, will keep customers loyal.

(8) The extra mile will have no traffic jams.

We sincerely hope we have helped motivate you to build your Cathedral! Good luck, God Bless, God Speed!

"I have fought the good fight, I have finished the race, I have kept the faith."

—2 Timothy 4:7

Cathedral Builder Reading List

- *The Bible*
- *I'm No Hero* by Captain Charles Plumb, USNR (Ret.)
- *My Enemy; My Friend* by Brigadier General Dan Cherry, USAF (Ret.)
- *Words for Warriors: A Professional Soldier's Notebook* by Colonel Ralph Puckett
- *Be-Know-Do: Leadership the Army Way* adapted from *The Official Army Leadership Manual*
- *The Emotional Intelligence Quick Book* by Travis Bradberry and Jean Greaves
- *Emotional Intelligence* by Daniel Goleman
- *The It Factor* by Mark Wiskup
- *Don't Give Up…Don't Ever Give Up: The Inspiration of Jimmy V* by Justin Spizman and Robin Spizman
- *The Leadership Challenge* by James Kouzes and Barry Posner
- *Tuesdays with Morrie* by Mitch Albom
- *Have a Little Faith* by Mitch Albom
- *Primal Leadership* by Daniel Goleman, Richard Boyatzis and Annie McKee
- *Becoming Stress Resistant* by Raymond Flannery Jr, M.D.
- *The Relaxation Response* by Herbert Benson, M.D.
- *Stress Without Distress* by Hans Selye, M.D.
- *Halftime* by Bob Buford
- *Fish* by Stephen Lundin, Harry Paul and John Christensen
- *First, Break All The Rules* by Marcus Buckingham and Curt Coffman
- *Good to Great* by Jim Collins

- *Jesus, Life Coach* by Laurie Beth Jones
- *Pillars of the Earth* by Ken Follett
- *John Adams* by David McCullough
- *See You at the Top* by Zig Ziglar
- *The Purpose Driven Life* by Rick Warren
- *The 360 Degree Leader* by John Maxwell

The Author

Greg Coker is the founder of The Cathedral Institute, a full-service leadership development and consulting firm focusing on empowering people, building teams, transforming organizations and changing the world. He has over 25 years experience as a senior-level manager with three different Fortune 500 companies, a government regulator, an elected official, and a statewide leader. His experience ranges from leading the training and development for over 80,000 employees to directing governmental affairs and public relations at both the state and federal level. Greg Coker received both his undergraduate and his masters degrees in Organizational Communication from Western Kentucky University. His clients include public education, business and industry, colleges and universities, nonprofit organizations and high-performance individuals who benefit from his executive/ life coaching. He travels across the country delivering the keynote speech and workshop, "Building Cathedrals: The Power of Purpose." He and his wife Nicki have two teenage children, Will and Abby, and live in Franklin, Kentucky.

Contributors

Terry Curtis Daniels is the Human Resource Manager for ITW in Gallatin, TN. He has over 20 years in human resource, leadership, and team dynamics and development. He has led seminars and training sessions with Myers-Briggs (MBTI), Hermann Brain Dominance Instrument (HBDI), Diversity and Inclusion, and many leadership and team dynamics sessions. In addition, he has been the senior pastor of the Loving Chapel Baptist Church in Franklin, KY for almost 20 years, and has been sought after to speak before many large audiences. He graduated from Western Kentucky University with a degree in Psychology and from Walden University with a degree in Organization Psychology and Development. Throughout his diverse background and wide range of activities, Terry has coached, counseled, trained, and mentored numerous individuals, teams, and organizations. He and his wife Rita and their three sons Tyler, Taylour, and Tanner reside in Bowling Green, KY.

Vincent "Skip" Wirth is the director of sales and marketing for First Choice Home Medical in Bowling Green, KY. He has over 38 years of healthcare experience in a variety of settings, including clinical, supervisory, education, sales, marketing and administration. He graduated with honors from Western Kentucky University with degrees in Nursing and Public Health, and has a master's degree in Organizational Communication. He is an adjunct faculty member at WKU in the Department of Speech and Communication. Throughout his career, Skip has presented to over 1,500 groups on stress management, wellness, team building, leadership, communication, customer service, and humor in the workplace. He and his wife Lynn are the proud parents of daughter Elizabeth.

Dave Tatman is the plant manager of the General Motors Bowling Green Assembly Plant, the world's only producer of the Chevrolet Corvette. In June 1978, Tatman began working for GM as a college intern. He has held numerous supervisory and management positions over a 12-year period before being transferred to Powertrain's Advanced Development Center in Pontiac as superintendent in Product Engineering. In 1995, Dave moved to the Powertrain plant in Bay City as a business team manager. From 1997 to 2000, Tatman held the position of manufacturing executive at GM of Canada. In January 2000, Tatman returned to Pontiac, working at Powertrain headquarters as the director of North American Manufacturing Quality Systems. In 2001, he moved to the Toledo Transmission plant as production manager and in 2004, was named plant manager of the Livonia Engine plant. He recently completed a seven-month assignment at Powertrain Operations in Sao Jose dos Campos, Brazil. Then, November 1, 2008, Tatman was named plant manager of the Willow Run Site, and on August 1, 2010, he added Warren Transmission and Parma to his responsibilities.

Tatman received a Bachelor of Science degree in Industrial Engineering from Ohio State University in June 1980 and a master's degree in Business Administration from the University of Michigan in December 1985. Dave and his wife Barbie have two grown sons, John and Phil. John, 23, lives and goes to school in Ann Arbor, MI, and Phil, 21, lives and goes to school in Bellingham, WA. Their daughter, Parke, is 17 and an enthusiastic hunter jumper equestrian.

The Artist

Faye Christian Phillips fell in love with art at the age of 10 when she first discovered Michelangelo in the pages of a book. As a child, she found the images of his sculptures and frescoes to be profoundly moving. It was an emotional connection that years later would lead her to Italy to see his work, and one that set her on a path to a life in art. After studying art in college, Faye narrowed her focus to painting years later with adventures in art, allowing her to study with some of the country's finest living artists.

As a member of Oil Painters of America, The American Impressionists Society, and the local Artworks organization, Faye continues to exhibit in regional and national shows as well as private commissions. Faye is married to J.K., and has three sons, two daughters-in-law and two grandchildren and lives in Bowling Green, KY. Faye's journal of her painting journey can be viewed at http://faye-christian-phillips.blogspot.com/.

A collection of works can be seen at http://web.me.com/fayzart/faye_christian_phillips_fine_art/.

"Building Cathedrals: The Power of Purpose"
Keynote Speech

Building Cathedrals: The Power of Purpose is based on a story that has been told for over 300 years and which illustrates that the most productive and successful people in life are those of purpose. While many have heard a version of this story, Greg Coker traced the origin of this life-changing story to the world's most famous architect, Christopher Wren. After the fire of 1666 that leveled London, Wren was commissioned to rebuild Saint Paul's Cathedral.

Greg Coker captivates audiences as he enriches this story, illuminating the leadership qualities of Christopher Wren, and revisiting the fire of 1666 and its redemptive qualities. Those qualities pertain not only to London but also in our personal lives as well. He introduces a powerful metaphor, a "Cathedral," as something that adds purpose to our lives and drives our behavior, while encouraging us to not only find our Cathedral, but also to help and support others in finding their Cathedrals. The "Bricklayers" in the story provide the backdrop for a rich discussion on employee engagement and the dynamics that occur in modern day organizations.

The highlight of the speech is the recounting of personal stories from people who are building modern-day Cathedrals, as well as those who have experienced "personal fires," but like London were able to come out stronger, quicker, and faster. Greg Coker concludes with a list of simple yet powerful examples of how we have the amazing power and the responsibility to touch and inspire others in a deep and meaningful way.

As a professional speaker, Greg Coker travels the country delivering this powerful speech in an entertaining and inspirational style to Fortune 500 companies, government agencies, trade associations, civic organizations, colleges and universities. His presentation, tailored especially for each organization, will inspire, motivate and move audiences through a range of emotions. The ultimate result is everyone leaving with a renewed commitment to one's purpose and a clearer understanding of the Cathedrals, both personal and organizational, that must be built.

Building Cathedrals: The Power of Purpose Workshop

This powerful workshop, based on Greg Coker's book and keynote speech, "Building Cathedrals: The Power of Purpose" is customized especially for you and your organization and is offered in both half-day and full-day sessions. While the book and the keynote speech are *motivational*, this workshop is *transformational*, focusing on six keys areas guaranteed to take your company from a culture of "Bricklayers" to a culture of "Cathedral Builders":

➤ Leadership

➤ Engagement

➤ Culture

➤ Purpose

> Customer Loyalty

> Teamwork

For more details, visit us at www.thecathedralinstitute.com today and start the Transformation!

About The Cathedral Institute

The Cathedral Institute is a full-service leadership development and consulting firm with a mission of empowering people, building teams, transforming organizations and changing the world. Our services include keynote speaking, training workshops, organization development, executive/life coaching, public relations, governmental affairs and management consulting. Our principals and associates have extensive backgrounds in both the public and private sector assisting and partnering with both domestic and international clients. For more information, please visit our website at www.thecathedralinstitute.com

The Cathedral Institute

1145 Bennington Place

Franklin, Kentucky 42134

(270) 223-8343

www.thecathedralinstitute.com

The Cathedral Institute: Empowering People, Developing Teams, Transforming Organizations, Changing the World